Invisible

NO MORE;

INVINCIBLE FOREVER MORE

Inspiring Stories of Women Who
Have Gone From Invisible
to Invincible

created by
LYNDA SUNSHINE WEST

Dedicated to all women who have fallen under hard
times in their lives making them feel invisible.
You are victorious!!

Women Action Takers™ Publishing
www.womenactiontakers.com

ebook ISBN: 978-1-7348759-5-9
Paperback ISBN: 978-1-7348759-4-2

Editorial services by Kristy Boyd Johnson of Turtle Sea Books
Cover Design by Ryanzzzz
Printed in the United States of America

Table of Contents

When your faith is strong, your fear is weakened.

Faith

Erases

Anxious

Reactions

~Lynda Sunshine West

A Sunny Note from Lynda Sunshine

Welcome to *Invisible No More; Invincible Forever More*! Since you've picked up this book, chances are you are a woman who has felt invisible at some point in your life, or you may be feeling invisible today. You may be feeling stuck while facing the fact that invisibility is real and you want out of it and want to step up and take charge of your life. This feels like a daunting challenge, but we're here for you.

We all need a boost every now and then to help us climb our personal mountains. There is no shame whatsoever in asking for help from an expert. The only shame, perhaps, is not receiving such a gift with gratitude when it is placed before us—whether we are able to follow the advice or not.

I've been blessed by connecting with amazing women who are making a positive impact on the planet by throwing caution to the wind and doing what they love. They are living their purpose and are loving every minute of it. If you're in a space where you're struggling with your business and aren't sure where to turn, I have your back—as do all of the wonderful contributors to this book. Know that there is a solution to every problem and someone knowledgeable in your circle of contacts is ready, willing, and able to help you. All you need to do is *ask*!

If you do happen to stumble backwards—as I have on more occasions than I care to admit—you must get right back up on your feet and learn from your experience. You will be amazed at how failure often leads to even greater opportunity and success down the road.

Why *Invisible No More; Invincible Forever More*?

During my journey, I have encountered feelings of being invisible to that point that, even if I was on stage, I felt alone. Those feelings of disbelief about myself led me down a lonely path. At age 51, I made the decision to reach out for help and found a life coach who led me on a journey of facing fears and realizing I have value. From the moment I realized I have value my entire life changed and I moved into a place of invincibility.

If this is you, then you know what I'm talking about. Well, you're in the right place because these authors are just like you.

My goal—which is shared among all of the contributors to this book—is to add all of our collective advice to help you grow and move yourself into the space of feeling invincible. When you feel invincible, nothing can stop you from achieving the life you want to live. We want to see you accomplish all of your dreams and goals and flourish.

What Is This Book About?

One morning I woke up and, before my feet hit the floor, God sent me a message saying, "You're going to write collaboration books with entrepreneurs to share their story. Their story has power and YOU are the one to get their message into the public." I heeded the word and stepped right into it.

The first book was titled *Momentum: 13 Lessons From Action Takers Who Changed the World*. Next, two titles came: *The Fearless*

Entrepreneurs and *Invisible No More; Invincible Forever More*. And, so, just like any other entrepreneurial endeavor, my journey began.

The main intent of this book is to spotlight the content of the contributors in a way that is accessible, actionable, and, hopefully, entertaining.

I would characterize this book as a compilation of journeys from women who have literally gone from feeling invisible, worthless, shamed, frightened, abused, etc. and changed their life to create the life they truly want to live. The mission is to provide lessons that are intended to help you address and problem-solve issues related to your life and your business.

The backgrounds and accomplishments of the contributors are all true. Their observations, principles, and lessons are 100% authentic to their life practices and philosophies. All of these brilliant individuals were an integral part of developing the content for this book. *Invisible No More; Invincible Forever More* would not have been possible without them. Please feel free to contact them via their websites—they would love to hear from you!

Welcome to our world.

Lynda Sunshine West
Founder, Women Action Takers

A Special Note About the Charity

100% of the net proceeds of the sales of this book will be donated to Dress for Success, a 501(c)(3) nonprofit charity that empowers women to achieve economic independence by providing a network of support, professional attire, and the development tools to help women thrive in work and in life. For further information or to make a donation, visit their website at www.dressforsuccess.org.

CHAPTER ONE

~

The Rising Sunshine

by Lynda Sunshine West
Founder, Women Action Takers™
www.WomenActionTakers.com

"Thank God! The bastard is dead." Those are the first words my mom said when my dad took his last breath.

We were in the hospital, standing about 20 feet away from his hospital bed.

Thursday night, he walked into the hospital having chest pain. Friday, after 86 heart attacks, around 4:00 p.m. he took his last breath.

I called him Dad, but really thought of him as a Monster all of my life. He was an abusive alcoholic and, even though he stopped drinking 40 years before he passed away, he was still that bastard mom referred to him as.

You may wonder why we allowed him to have 86 heart attacks before turning off his pacemaker.

Well, Mom was in charge and for the 55 years they were together, every decision Mom made was "wrong." She was so wrapped up in being wrong and making the wrong decisions, that she didn't want to tell the doctor to turn off his pacemaker. What a double-bind, indeed.

My husband and I arrived at the hospital around 3:00 p.m. We had no idea he had had so many heart attacks.

No matter how much I hated him, I didn't want to see him suffer like that.

Finally, I looked Mom in the eyes and said, "Mom, you gotta tell the doctor to turn off the pacemaker. It's time to let Dad go."

She said, "You do it. I can't."

And so I did.

When the doctor walked in, I gave him permission to turn it off, then stepped back to stand next to Mom. And we waited for him to take his last breath. The whole family was there, including my niece, nephew, daughter, and one friend of Dad's.

He finally took his last breath and the doctor pronounced him dead.

Mom said in a whisper loud enough for my husband and me to hear, "Thank God! The bastard is dead."

Normally, when someone passes away, you imagine people weeping, overwhelmed with grief and sadness. That wasn't the case in this hospital room. Only one person started crying. It was surreal. Dad's friend, whom he knew for more than 20 years from Alcoholics Anonymous, looked around the room and was dumbfounded. I can imagine him saying to himself, "What is going on? It's like Twilight Zone. No one is crying. No one is walking over to him to pay their respects. No one is saying anything."

I signed the paperwork and we walked out of the room. The "transaction" was complete. It was bizarre, but not surprising.

When we got downstairs, Mom said, "Dad and I didn't tell you this because we didn't want to worry you, but I have cancer."

What? Dad just died and you're telling us this now? Couldn't you wait a day?

With the way my life went, my immediate thought was terrible. I'm embarrassed to admit it, but this is the truth. My first thought was, "Now that he's gone, you're going to jump right into the spotlight?"

Since this is my story of going from invisible to Invincible, I want to mention how I am now a successful entrepreneur. I facilitate a large mastermind for women. I have interviewed stars on the Red Carpet and have done more than 4,000 live videos, interviewing more than 500 people (and counting). I publish collaboration books (including this one!) that are very well received and am a seven-time bestselling author in my own right. I live an inspired life and am a motivational speaker. This is my invincible part. That's the happy ending! Yet how did I move from an alcoholic abusive father, through an emotionally abusive first marriage, and finally to an endless state of Invincibility? After escaping my childhood home, how did I survive being yelled at every day by the man who "loved" me? He would taunt me with such cruelty, saying, "You're so stupid. You're so ignorant. People are only nice to you because they feel sorry for you." How did I navigate out of believing him and carrying it around with me for several decades? No matter how much other people said great things about me, I still believed I was stupid and ignorant.

I married my first husband because I got pregnant. Mom pleaded with me, "You have to marry him. Dad can't know that you had sex before you were married." So, that's what I did. I got married. Not for love, and actually, not even because I was pregnant. The decision to get married when I was only 19 was all tied up in the fear I held of my dad.

One poignant day, my husband was yelling at me in front of the kids. This was usual. But what was not usual was that I stood up to him. I said, "If you want these kids to hate you as much as I hate my dad, then I'll stay with you." Looking back, I realize how irrational of a statement that was. But my body and mind were in such a constant state of turmoil, it was the best I could come up with.

On "moving day," I waited until he was out of the house and then I ran away.

I was 21 with my 4-week-old baby girl in the carrier, my 14-month-old baby boy on my hip, diaper bag over my left shoulder, and my purse over my right. I walked out, literally, because I had no car.

I knew in that moment, I was not going to live my mom's life.

I walked the four blocks to my parents' house.

A few weeks later, we were at the horse races. Dad was a huge gambler. Never a winner, but always a gambler. When he went to place his bets, Mom admonished me, "You can't divorce him. You have to stay together 'for the kids.'" Her words cut me like a knife. Time seemed to stand still as we sat in the warm sunshine of San Diego's Del Mar Racetrack, eating our picnic on the grass. I could not keep my thoughts to myself. They tumbled out with deep conviction, "I am not going to live your life, Mom. I am leaving FOR THE KIDS." Ouch! There, I said it.

This story really starts back when I was 5 and ran away from home. I was gone an entire week. Where did I go? That's the first question most people ask me. But that's certainly not the most important question. What could compel an innocent little five-year-old girl to run away for so long?

It was an extremely volatile household, filled with alcohol and abuse. Fear ran rampant in my childhood. Why did I run away? I decided in my pure innocent wisdom that I was *not* going to live in that house anymore. With those people. So I ran away to the safety of the neighbor's house. It made no difference that it was only two houses away. For all intents and purposes, it was a world away from my house. And I was planning to be gone forever. I never wanted to go back.

After a week, my mom brought me home. And what happened at my return is something that would shape the way I lived my life for decades to come. I came home with my tail between my legs and my head hung low. I refused to look anyone in the eye for many years.

I was riddled with fear.

As a teenager, I started working at your typical fast food minimum wage job at Carl's Jr. Over the next 36 years, I worked in 49 different corporate positions! Can anyone top that? Yet, I was never fired. I would get bored, feel under-appreciated, and would just move on to something new. Forty-nine times! I guess you can say I wasn't afraid of change!

As I look back on my work career, I realize my job hopping was a survival pattern that started when I was that 5-year-old little girl. I could just move on when things were not to my liking. I clearly remember one particular day when I was driving to job #49. I was a Legal Secretary to the #2 judge in the Ninth Circuit Court of Appeals. This was the penultimate job for me. I had been a legal secretary for 20 years and I had finally "made it." I began asking myself the quintessential questions. What is the purpose of this planet? What is my purpose on this planet? I was 51 years old and I was going to figure out what I wanted to do with my life.

My answers would come through a life coach. Hiring her is one of the best gifts I have ever given myself. Working with her helped me to discover who I really am, what value I have to offer, and who I can serve.

I wish those answers came as fast as I just typed that previous sentence! It actually took nearly five years before I could begin to completely and fully answer those questions. It has been an amazing journey and, in many ways, I am still on the journey. I am grateful to that coach for helping me make those discoveries which put me on the path to entrepreneurship. I am deeply grateful to myself for raising my hand and saying, "I deserve this. I am worthy." This is where my "invincibility" story begins to reveal itself.

On New Year's Day 2015, I decided I was going to do things differently. This declaration came on the heels of an epiphany I had at the end of 2014 when I said, "I am going to quit my job and become an entrepreneur. I'm going to become a millionaire in a year." In the face of the grim statistics that most entrepreneurs fail in the first two years of business, I was determined to beat those odds. I was not about to fail at this. I had spent 36 miserable years working for other people and I knew I was not going to back to that! I would not go back. I was determined to succeed.

Even with the profound transformations I experienced working with my life coach, I acutely recognized that fear was stopping me from living the life I wanted. Fear, in all of its millions of varieties, had blocked me from doing so many things I dreamed of, including running my own business. I felt paralyzed when trying to take action. I was haunted by the risk of failing so much so that I would not even try. I just could not stomach "returning home" a failure like when I was 5 and, again, when I was 21.

Then it hit me! I decided to stop running from those fears and, instead, face them head-on. I created a personal challenge: to face a fear every single day for the entire year of 2015. The time had come for me to take my power back.

It went something like this . . . the first thing I would do every morning was to ask myself, "What scares me?" Then I stayed in bed waiting for the answer to come. The FIRST fear that came into my mind was the fear I "committed" to breaking through that day. This wasn't a New Year's Resolution. This was a COMMITMENT to change. A COMMITMENT to myself. I asked this ONE question 365 days in a row. And it changed my life.

Being an entrepreneur is the perfect laboratory for facing 365 fears (and more)! The uncertainty of entrepreneurship is daunting, even terrifying. I was that person at networking events who would sit in the back corner, head buried in my phone. I was too anxious to start a conversation. My mind would go blank if someone started a conversation with me. I was too scared to raise my hand and offer a comment or ask a question. I felt paralyzed trying to use my voice. I realized these behaviors were deeply rooted in the master fear: the fear of judgment. What if I say the wrong thing? What if I sound ignorant? What if I make a fool of myself? So many "what if's." And so I would queue up another round of solitaire on my phone.

The abusive environment of my childhood kept a stranglehold on me. No matter how well I did, my traumas kept overpowering me. I continued to believe I was stupid and just plain ignorant. I know some people who grew up in a similar environment and they are able to use the abuse to fuel them to do better. That wasn't my story, though. I felt shriveled up and small and so disbelieving in myself. I chose that story until I went through my personal transformation and self re-discovery. Remember how strong and brave I was at five years old?! I was becoming that take-charge little girl again. I decided on a new storyline for the life ahead of me: I was now accepting full responsibility for my actions and for my life. I was done blaming my childhood for the decisions I was making today. This included the abuse, the alcohol, my mom, my dad, my ex-husband. I was done blaming them for everything amiss in my life today.

I read in Jack Canfield's book, "The Success Principles," that the first principle of success is to take 100% responsibility for your life and actions. That hit me hard. It was actually my wake-up call to the fact that I had been making a lot of excuses as to why I wasn't living the life I desired. Blaming others is the exact antithesis for taking responsibility for one's self. Once I started accepting responsibility for my own actions, doors opened and my life changed even more. Facing a fear everyday was simply the tool I chose to use in order to step into my new life, my brilliance, my confidence, my growth, and my self. My True Self.

On a random morning, the answer to my daily question, "What scares me?" was extremely specific: approach and talk to a stranger in

Starbucks. I had used Starbucks as a remote office like many entrepreneurs. I would quickly pull out my laptop, start working, and definitely not make eye contact with anyone. While it may seem like a small, even silly fear, it was actually a crippling fear for me. Fear is fear. My decision to face a fear every day for a year was a commitment to myself for growth. And, boy, how I grew!

Back at Starbucks, I was standing in a corner, watching people come in, place their order, and leave with their coffee. One man came in, placed his order, and then he sat down. My victim! My target was a person sitting alone so I could have a conversation with them. And there he was: alone, sitting, waiting for his coffee. I was finally going to face this fear. I stood there, staring at him, desperately trying to come up with my opening line of the conversation.

After he picked up his coffee and returned to his table, I slowly walked over to him, knees trembling, throat locked up, palms and forehead sweaty, stomach all knotted up. Praying my voice would not fail me, I managed to say, "Hi, sir. I'm facing a fear every day this year. And today's fear is to talk to a stranger in Starbucks." He responded suspiciously good-humored, "Okay!?"

So far, so good. I got the words out of my mouth in a coherent manner and he responded.

"Do you mind if I have a seat?"

"Sure. Please have a seat."

I chatted with him for about five minutes, stood up and said, "Thank you for your time. You helped me break through this fear. I appreciate it." I turned and walked out of Starbucks. I felt like throwing up. But I didn't.

I'm often asked, "Is Sunshine your real name?" No, it isn't.

During this personal development journey, I have changed drastically and have become a completely different person (happier and full of positive energy). Sunshine is not my given name. It is not even a nickname from my childhood. It is the name that was given to me during my personal development journey. Several years after working with my life coach, random people started calling me "Sunshine." It felt weird at first because I did not feel anything like "Sunshine." After the third person called me this, I took my own advice: "See yourself through the eyes of others, for others see the real you." I adopted the name "Lynda Sunshine West," changed all of my social media and embarked on the journey of believing myself to be "Sunshine." Pure, radiant Sunshine.

I believe we are all born with brilliance inside of us. While it seems like it took a while to tap into it, I feel it was necessary the way it unfolded so I would have compassion for those going through what I went through. I get it now. My journey is my journey. I wouldn't change it for the world. It has been an amazing ride . . . and it ain't over yet! I am fired up about the future, even though I have no idea just how marvelously it will all unfold. I have stopped running away. Now I run toward the future. I have stopped being ruled by fear. Now I am empowered and inspired by the smallest inkling of fear. I take actions BECAUSE I am scared. Go ahead and judge me for that!

CHAPTER TWO

~

From Geek to Chic: the Story of Forbes

by Forbes Riley

The Queen of Pitch and Celebrity Entrepreneur

http://forbesriley.com

You may not believe this from looking at me now, but I was a geeky, awkward child, the kind of kid who is truly invisible. I was overweight, with frizzy hair, a broken nose, and no friends. But I did have one redeeming quality: I was qualified as a genius. Trust me, this is not fun. I didn't relate to people. Any time I was in public, it was painful. Even still, I was a very scrappy kind of girl.

At home, I was a princess. My parents adored me. They understood me. I never had to explain who I was. My dad was a bigger geek than I was. We built a computer when I was eighteen years old. We did magic tricks. We would take things apart and tinker with them to see how they worked. We used to hop on the CB radio, and we even shot guns in the garage. Really crazy stuff. We were geeky together and that was okay.

My mother was an only child of immigrants from Russia. Her dad was a butcher. Her mom – my grandmother – was five-foot-two, this tiny little thing, and a bookie who raised bulldogs. Do you imagine this woman and my mom would have a lot of money? Not really. My mom, an only child, was five-foot-nine and slept on the couch. Never had her own bedroom. My grandma and I shared a bedroom and then one day, my grandma was gone. She passed away in her sleep.

We were this odd, tight-knit family and we loved each other.

When I was four years old, my sister was born. I walked into the bedroom one day to find my mom crying. Here she was, with a newborn and a really precocious four-year-old on her hands. We used to go to the cemetery and visit her parents and she would cry. She was never as happy as she was before they passed away. And she always used to romanticize that my grandma died of a broken heart because my grandpa had just died of leukemia. My mom cried a lot after her parents passed away. I spent a lot of time, most of my childhood in fact, trying to make her happy.

And we grew up in the kitchen. Everything in our world was about food. We ate. We ate when we were happy, sad, anything. And it was always sugar-based: Frosted Flakes and milk, maybe a glass of orange juice, which is also just sugar, for breakfast. Then we had lunch, usually a bologna sandwich on white bread with a snack of some sort, like a Yodel. Oh my God, we loved those yummy Yodels, but they were really just crap wrapped in fake chocolate. Then dinner was chicken-fried cutlets, mashed potatoes, canned beans, and always dessert "because we love you." My mom was 260 pounds. I had huge thighs. And then, when we went out, we would go to the new, big deal McDonald's in town. There was not an ounce of nutrition in my childhood.

And so I entered high school as a pudgy girl. I remember my two high school girlfriends. They could both sing, they were both pretty, and they always had the leads in school plays. It was kind of sad for me.

I always wanted to be an actress. I wanted to be Julia Roberts or Sandra Bullock. That career path looked really appealing to me. I wanted to be the pretty girl up on that stage. I wanted to be the lead. I auditioned all the time and I never got anything. I got number three, or in the chorus, or the role of the chicken.

Sigh.

When I went off to college, I planned to be a lawyer because that's what smart kids did in my world. You were either a doctor or a lawyer – there was no other option. I didn't know what "CEO" meant.

In college, I put myself out there because I always wanted to matter. I auditioned for Shakespeare's *As You Like It*. I'm not that good at English, but I still got up there and auditioned. I went to look at the call board and I immediately looked at the bottom, which is where I always lived. And I spotted my name... cast in the role of Rosalind. I thought, "Two and a half hours on stage playing the most amazing character Shakespeare ever wrote for a woman. Me. Woo. Oh my God."

My first reaction was like, "I have to go talk to the director because why would he do that?" I know that sounds really stupid, right? I went to Professor David Wichmann, my acting teacher, and said, "Explain this to me. I don't know if I can do this."

He sat me down and said, "You have so much depth, so much passion, so much empathy, so much pain." He went on and on, but it seemed to me as if he were talking about somebody else. I should mention, this man was 100% legally blind. He couldn't see all the exterior stuff that stopped people from seeing what he saw – the real person inside me. He saw into my heart.

That was an amazing experience. And it went deep. At last I had the social proof – I could do this!

But then I had to tell my mom that I didn't want to be a lawyer. I didn't want to go against my parents. I grew up always wanting to please my parents and get their love. But I went ahead and did it anyway.

It was a big deal for me to tell them, but they surprised me. They told me they never wanted me to be a lawyer in the first place. They didn't care that I had changed my mind. They just wanted me to be happy. They gave me their blessing. They said, "Go for it. We love you. We're going to support whatever you do."

I realized I had built up a bizarre story in my head that was never real. They were the most amazing, supportive people in the world. I don't know why I would've thought any different. I learned a little lesson about me in this journey.

Everything changed after that.

I didn't know what the outcome would be or worry about what could happen, but I moved to New York without even knowing where I was going to live. But you know what happened? I landed the lead role in the first movie for which I auditioned, a now-cult classic called *Splatter University*. I also did more films, some Broadway, and soap operas.

Even though I was putting myself out there, I was dealing with my own weight issues that whole time. I'd be on Broadway with Christopher Reeve, then head to an Overeaters Anonymous meeting afterwards. It was always like this double-edged sword. I couldn't quite believe I was really deserving of all this. Even though I struggled, I still did what I did and just leaped and let stuff happen. Looking back in my career, I didn't plan any of it.

Let me tell you a story: late one night, I got a phone call. I was asked to be in a celebrity cookbook, and I had to deliver *right then* because the deadline was the next day. Someone had literally dropped out that night. This amazing woman called and said, "Can you put five of your favorite recipes together, with high res pictures, and get them to me by tomorrow?"

So I grabbed a girlfriend of mine who was a chef. She came over at 10 o'clock that night. There we were cooking, with the cameras rolling.

You could watch it on the Instagram Live because I have a habit of just throwing my hat into the ring and figuring out how to do it later.

That's the message: you don't have to know how to speak or dance or drive. Just go do it. You'll figure it out. If your journey is to figure out who you are and your place in this world, if you want to help others, you do have to put your metaphorical mask on first.

The second thing is this: I don't have a whole lot of time for the gym, but I wanted an amazing body. I wanted sexy arms, but I never had them before I started to use my little SpinGym. Seriously, if you do the routine three times a day for one month, your life, your arms, your body, your attitude, and your energy will be aligned with what you want. You don't need to go to the gym. SpinGym is the only thing I know that doubles your heartrate.

I'll tell you what – I spent a lot of my life promoting this product for people who were in wheelchairs, stuck in the office, super fit, or not super fit, at every age. This is the dream product. I just want people to understand and know what this is, because if you found something so wonderful, wouldn't you want to share it, too?

And it's amazing because what I finally have realized, after many years of having money issues, is this: if we're not telling people about what we have, then they're not going to know about it. It's not at all self-serving – it's the opposite. Why? Because if you don't introduce it to them, they're not going to know about it, and it's not going to be able to change their lives.

It's really about them.

The last thing is: you have to know what you want, in very specific terms. Your wants have to be actionable, measurable, and quantifiable. There's a clarity to this. If you can **know** what you want, you can truly manifest it. When I wanted Joshua and I finally got clear what I wanted, the life partner appeared.

Here's what happened: I was actually brazen enough to write down that I wanted someone who looked like he walked off the cover of a romance novel. I didn't go on Tinder. I didn't do a dating app. I didn't go to a bar. I just wrote it down. And in my own crazy vision, he knocked on my door of my hotel room to be a SpinGym model, the product that I love.

And then it happened. He changed my entire life because I wanted it.

For me, the discovery was the details. We have to understand the difference. I'm an odd, awkward introvert (this is not a joke). It is what keeps me from a lot of things. People invite me to things, but I tend not to go. I go when it's important. For example, I'll do red carpets. I love to speak in front of other people. Obviously, my Facebook presence is outgoing and looks a certain way. That's not really who I am. That's who I have to be to function.

Here's what I've learned. I am at a certain age. I admit this and say, "I am six months away from sixty years old." Well, I have to say, I look good for forty-five or fifty. I look amazing, but sixty? Oh yeah. But it is becoming more and more of a reality. I almost don't want to say the age because everyone has this weird stigma about it. I do too. So, I'm not sure how I'm supposed to feel about this, especially as a woman. But I have to face the reality and tell myself, "That is this age, this number, and congratulations for fixing enough in my life to look like this at this age."

It's a truth that things happen. Bad things will happen to you. We age. People you love will die. You will break things. You will suffer hardships from time to time. You're going to die. So ask yourself, "What am I doing here? How much time do I have? How much fun can I have?" For me, I have a lot of fun standing on stages. I have a lot of fun acting. I'm going to go do more of that. I have a lot of fun watching my kids grow up. You have to enjoy this life as if it were the only one you've got.

Now there are a couple of things that I hear people say that are wrong, and the biggest one is that everything happens for a reason. That would mean that somebody is up there with a scorecard. That's just silly.

What's true is that, if you walk around whining, "Oh, why me?" I'm going to answer, "Why? You've gotta be kidding me. What do you mean, why?" Things happen, but you can find your purpose within the experience. I'm inspired when I look at Pedro, who's in one of my videos for SpinGym. He had his arms and legs amputated. At first, he sat around going, "Why me?" Now he reasons that he got a second chance in life. And his job is now to inspire people. And he has a massive platform. He doesn't hold himself back by asking why. He just moves forward.

I have a girlfriend, who's a little person. She is three foot, two inches tall. She walked around the first part of her life, whining, "Why? Why me? Why am I so different?"

I looked at her and said, "Why not? Girlfriend, everybody remembers you. You're adorable and cute and fit. You walk into a room, and everyone knows you. All of us who are trying to be famous would love that opportunity." Let's start switching the messaging we're giving ourselves, the self-talk, and just get happier.

I've gotten to a certain level of success, a certain level of fame, and I feel it's important for me to give back and inspire others. Because if you're suffering like I did (and I know you are), I know what that is. I know what it's like when the door closes and there's nobody. Or you had dreams of being something where your heart got broken, or you didn't get that job, or you got fired, or nobody loves you. You surely don't know these life lessons at my kids' age of sixteen/seventeen, but you do. You get to a certain point where you have more years behind you than you do ahead of you. That is pretty much a guarantee. I have more youth behind me than ahead of me. And so now I understand what we all are looking for. There is a level of self-acceptance that you have to find, and there are a lot of ways to find it. But if you find your truth, life is better. There are too many people who won't bother. And I'll tell you what, what we're seeing in society right now is people who take out guns and threaten to kill because they can't handle it anymore. I understand. Life will push you to those points.

Here's what you've got to understand: you cannot read somebody else's mind. You have no idea what somebody else is thinking. One of my coaching clients was in his forties, but he had not told his mom that he was gay. He was freaking out about coming out of the closet. And we're all looking at him, thinking, "You know, it's not real secret."

Still, he said, "I can't tell my parents I'm gay." He was terrified. I coached him to actually tell her, and he did. He had a breakthrough and now he's happier than ever.

A couple things about seminars. I didn't know until I went to my first one at age thirty-one what they could do for you. I was so obsessed about money because we had none. My dad spent three years in the hospital. He had a horrible industrial accident. And so money had been an issue for me. This first seminar cost $500 – and back then, that was a LOT of money. For some people, it's still a lot of money.

At that time, I didn't want to spend it. But here's the thing: you've got to invest in yourself. Until you do it, you'll never know those of us who are successful and have invested hundreds of thousands of dollars. The more famous somebody is, the more wealthy. And you know, they've had some pretty serious training. Think about how much you invested in college.

I had this friend who offered to pay for my attendance at a seminar. I thought, "Oh great. He's going to want to sleep with me." In my brain, nobody gives you anything for free without expecting something in return.

But that was never the case. It was just his gift, his generosity, and a different relationship with money. He had a mindset of prosperity. I went to that seminar and it changed my life. I did the training for five days. I learned things in this class. It was unbelievable. Then on the way out, they tried to upsell us the next level course, which was $900.

My reaction was less than positive. I got on the phone with this generous person and said, "See, I told you, they're always just trying to sell you something. And I'm not going to pay for that."

"Didn't you just have a breakthrough in the five days?" he asked me.

I paused, and said, "Oh my God, it was amazing."

"So what's the real problem?" he said. "You're still dealing with issues. You have to understand, acknowledge your own issues. They will do healing for you." And then this amazing person said, "Tell you what. I'll give you a loan. You make the terms."

I said, "How about a hundred dollars a month for nine months? No interest."

"Done."

Here's what I want to tell you guys. The Saturday night of that training week still remains one of the top five nights of my entire life. Here's what happened: they broke us up into small groups and assigned a song to perform on stage for each group. My group had four people. I was so excited! I love doing stuff like this! So when they got to my group and said, "You four will put on server's outfits. For the rest of the evening, it's your job to serve food, clean up, and just generally be at our beck and call," well, you can imagine my disappointment.

I was angry too, but I did it.

At the end, they brought the four of us who served onto the stage, blindfolded and barefoot. When they removed the blindfolds, the four coaches were washing our feet. Everyone else in the room was on the floor, bowing to us.

The message? "You are natural leaders, but in order to learn to lead, you must first learn to serve."

Had I not given in to what I understand now was a limiting belief that came from my parents, I would never have had that incredible, life-changing experience.

That training is one reason that I teach my seminars now, because I know how profoundly the entire trajectory of my life changed in that moment. I do this for other people because it's so precious. It's so spectacular. I would not be here or anywhere near here if I hadn't done that first.

You may be thinking that seminars don't work. Maybe the first five seminars that you attended didn't work for you. Who cares? There IS something out there, but if you stop looking and stop bettering yourself, you won't find it. You won't shift to the next level. As a professional entrepreneur, you should always have continuing ed classes. We take courses as an entrepreneur, as a small business owner, as a human being, because it's really, really important to grow.

I'm here to tell you that if you're willing to risk who you are, and own who you are, what's on the other side of that is unbelievable. It's a beautiful place and you'll never regret making that leap. I'm living proof you can transform your life no matter what your circumstances, even if you think you're invisible.

Here's the thing: there is no end. There is just the journey. So
you GOT to enjoy it.
— Forbes Riley

CHAPTER THREE

~

Be the Hero of Your Own Life's Story

by Rachele Brooke Smith
Actress, Filmmaker, Host, Speaker & Coach
https://rachelebsmith.com

Disrupt doubt. Be your own hero.
— **Rachele Brooke Smith**

I grew up as a competitive gymnast. If you did intense sports as a child, you know the kind of constant pressure there is to perform. If one of my coaches yelled at me, which happened a lot, I took it as "I am a failure." There was no middle ground for me like there seemed to be for my teammates. I was a high achiever and put a ton of extra stress on my body, my mind, and my spirit. I lived in a near-constant state of worry, fear, and anxiety under all the pressure I put on myself to be The Best.

The stress became so severe that I would stay home sick about half the time. I would crave "being sick" so I could stay home with my mom, who was my best friend, all cuddled up in my bed. It was the only way

I ever felt safe. I was throwing up on a weekly basis, not from an eating disorder, but because of the constant, unending anxiety. This started when I was about age eight and continued for four years.

Four *years*.

One day, during a competition, I broke my hand. Although it was painful, it was also a relief. The broken hand and subsequent surgery made me be still and quiet. For six months, I was able to go to practice and just condition... without all the pressure. This opened up a whole new way of experiencing life. I got a taste of what it was like to live without all the stress and fear, but I still got to be around my friends, and everyone was happy. It was the best of both worlds.

When my hand healed and it was time to go back, every part of my Being screamed no! Yet, the fear of change nearly made me stick in there in spite of my desperation. Even thinking about quitting sent me into a spiral of depression. I felt like I was losing my goals, my passion, my purpose. Worse, what about my friends? How would our relationships change if I was no longer "part of the team?" It was ridiculously hard for me to even think about saying the words "I quit" to my coach... much less my mom. I spent countless days locked in my room, crying, alone, scared, helpless. I'll never forget that struggle with such conflicting feelings.

I worked up the courage to tell my mom that I wanted to quit. Her reaction? "I don't like you right now. I can't be around you for a while."

To have my mom express such disappointment to me... well, let's just say I cried in my room for a long time. Worse still, my friends reacted pretty much the same. They seemed to feel I had somehow betrayed them. But I had to quit. I just couldn't take it anymore.

A short time later, I saw the movie *Center Stage*, directed by Nicholas Hytner. It's the story of young dancers in [the fictitious] American Ballet Company in New York. It explores the stress that these dancers experience and how they deal with the pressure. The main character is constantly being told "she can't." She doesn't have what it takes… or the right body type… she'll never be anything. But ultimately, she finds her own innovative way to create something better than she ever imagined.

I was completely riveted by the performance. It awakened something deep in my soul. I stayed in the theater long after it was over, crying and praying and visualizing myself as an actor and a dancer. My family actually had to come and find me and pull me out of the theater.

I left the theater that day a changed person, filled with joy and wonder. All the fear, loneliness, and anxiety were gone. I had discovered my purpose at last. I knew beyond any doubt that I wanted to act and tell stories about overcoming struggle. I wanted to challenge people, make them laugh, to dance and perform for them. But mostly, I wanted to inspire and change lives, just as those actors in the film had done for me. My love of movies rose to the level of obsession because I realized how powerful they could be.

My mind was set on this new path. I kept saying, "This is what I want to do. I want to dance." It took a while, but my mom came around. She saw that my enthusiasm wasn't going away, and she wanted me to be happy and do something I loved. This was a huge transformation for my mom as well. She found the joy of watching her kids discover their joy.

We started looking at dance studios, seeking out the best ones to audition for or join. I started acting classes. Before long, my joy became contagious. And boy, did my life shift. I ate, drank, and *breathed* dance and acting. At last, I felt free. I had rediscovered a sense of joy within myself, and my mom was my biggest supporter of the dream.

Interestingly enough, she made me a promise to never get so invested again, as she had done with my gymnastics career. She realized how unhealthy that was, and how much unconscious pressure that put on both of us. Now, of course, she is my number one superfan.

I was still plagued by perfectionism, and still put a ton of pressure on myself, but here's the thing: I wasn't living in fear anymore. I lived for my absolute love of movement, creativity, and storytelling. And even though I was plagued by bodily stiffness from years of gymnastics training, it was still one of the happiest times in my life.

You see, I just kept believing that story from *Center Stage*, that hero's journey. The things that happened to the main character seemed like "bad" things: not getting accepted into the Academy, being told she wasn't good enough, and so forth, ended up being the best things that happened to her. I was so inspired by the idea that she did it anyway – that she could overcome anything. "If she could do it, so can I," I thought.

I began to devour books, videos, pretty much any kind of educational materials or content that would help me get through my feelings of discouragement, defeat, doubt, and help me understand that my negative fear-thoughts didn't really matter. It was what I thought of myself that affected my emotions, and it was the way I *felt about myself* that really mattered. My feelings affected the next steps I took, my reactions to situations, and that would affect my opportunities and the possibilities that came to me in my life. I began to wonder how many people stay with things that make them unhappy because they fear change.

It took a long time before anyone gave me a shot. All that time, I kept the flame of "I know I'm good" alive in my heart. I barely slept all through high school. I even got the "Rat Award" at my studio because I would stay and practice well after my five hours of daily classes were over.

I worked my buns off to meet my goal of attending my dream college, with one of the best performing arts programs, with the future goal to move on to LA to pursue my dream of being a lead actress. I had the grades, I had everything I needed.

But my plan failed.

I was not a shoo-in, as I had thought, to my dream college. I just didn't get in.

So, I applied to ASU. It seemed like the signs were pointing me in that direction – all my friends were going there, and I received a scholarship, much to the delight of my father.

But there was this little nagging voice in my head. My heart just wasn't in this. *Could there be a better way?* I wondered.

Then, like a detour appearing in the road, an opportunity for a scholarship to attend a super-intense performing arts program in LA dropped out of the sky and into my lap.

I jumped on it. I begged my mom to take me to the audition. She finally agreed.

My mom and I flew to LA. There were literally thousands of kids from all over the world there to audition, but I was one of the eighteen who won the scholarship. I was in! Suddenly, the worst thing that had ever happened to me became the best thing that had ever NOT happened for me.

The big surprise came when I found out I only had two weeks to move to LA and be all set up and ready to go. That was freakin' scary. I had just graduated from high school, and I didn't know anyone in LA. There was a lot to figure out, but I knew I could do it.

Then we broke the news to my dad.

"No," he said. "This isn't the way. You have to go to college first. Then you can do what you want."

It was a big fight. He was scared for his daughter, and he wanted to do the right thing, too. My mom understood how important and amazing this opportunity was for me, and we finally talked him into it, as long as I agreed to get my college degree online while I was doing this "new thing."

And it all worked out. Looking back, that program was one of the most difficult things I ever did. It was six days a week, all day long. There were no excuses, no sick days, no vacation days. It didn't matter that I was only eighteen and living in a strange place, and so homesick and scared that I cried myself to sleep nearly every night. If I missed a day for any reason, I had to make it up. The toughest class was called "Hollywood." It went from 9am to 7pm every day and was the most physically and emotionally challenging class I ever had.

In spite of the trials, I LOVED it! I kept my vision board up to remind myself why I was working so hard to do this "impossible" thing.

Even now, I sometimes wish I could go back there, where all I had to do was show up for class and never worry about auditioning. During that time, we were not allowed to have an agent or work in any form of the entertainment industry. We were not allowed distractions that might take us out of our training.

As soon as I finished training, I crushed a performance which had some amazing dance agents present. I was signed immediately, but I knew I also needed an acting agent. My dream was to dance AND act. I tried to get signed with an acting agency, but my lack of a reel stood in my way. After all, how could I have a reel after being in an intensive dance academy where we weren't allowed to audition? I was turned down again and again and I was feeling pretty discouraged.

I had taught myself that, when I felt discouraged, to go dance. So I did what I had taught myself to do. I screamed and cried and prayed and moved my body. It always made me feel better.

I came out of my dance room and synchronicity happened. I spotted a sign on the wall announcing auditions for the lead female role in *Center Stage: Turn It Up*, the sequel to the very film which had changed my life. My jaw dropped and my heart skipped a beat.

There's never been any kind of announcement here ever before, I thought. *Am I being punked?* I felt so small and so not good enough from all the rejection, but another part of me was screaming, "This is it! Gotta jump on this!"

My head spun with the surrealness of it all. This was my dream movie, being cast at the exact moment when I could finally audition and was fully prepared? Talk about right place, right time.

And then the negative self-talk started. You know those really dramatic moments you have with yourself in the mirror? Mine went something like, "I shouldn't even go. I've never even had an acting audition before. All those agents turned me down for a reason. How ready could I actually be?"

Have you ever noticed that we always have these two voices within us? One says, "Yes! Go for it!" and the other says, "Who are you to do anything?" It's up to us, every single day, to choose. Are we going to choose faith, and opportunity, and possibility? Or are we going to choose fear? Because that's all it is.

In spite of this deep anxiety, something just seemed to push me out the door. I felt compelled to go, regardless of all the doubts and fears that clouded my thinking.

I ended up being called back to audition six different times. It was a rollercoaster ride of crazy emotions, sleepless nights, and tears. I felt like my childhood dream was right there, within my grasp, yet at the same time, sickeningly far out of reach.

About a month after my initial audition, the call came, ironically from an agent who had once turned me down. She said, "Sony has offered you the role of Kate Parker."

I was literally being offered the lead in the sequel to the movie that had completely changed my life. I didn't even know how to handle that kind of news. I rushed to pack my bags because I had only two days to be ready to leave for two months of shooting in Vancouver.

The entire experience felt like a miracle. To this day, I am overwhelmingly grateful for the role that shaped my career and business.

If that's not a story of how to create whatever we want in this world, I don't know what is.

Every single film role or opportunity I've had in my life came because I was brave enough to say, "This is what I want to do," tell everyone about it, and not give in, never give in to discouragement or defeat.

I decide every day to disrupt the doubt and fear and limiting beliefs that hold me back from doing what I want to do, and instead choose the power within me, and to have faith in my ability to do incredible things.

What is the thing you have been working toward your whole life? The thing that you visualized, wrote down, kept believing in regardless of how hard, how challenged, or how discouraged you got?

We don't have to live on autopilot, just going through the motions. Every day, I choose to take charge of my life. No one is going to come and save me. It's up to me to be the author of my own life story, the hero of my own journey.

You have to be the one to look deep inside you and find ways to figure it out. I believe in this so much that I started my brand Disruptive Apparel. I started the movement to help people disrupt doubt and fear and limiting beliefs and decide to become their own hero.

I've learned so much that I've conditioned myself that, when I feel fear, I go ahead and do it anyway. I want everyone out there to know that, if you're going through a challenging time, you can lean on my belief that you are more than enough. If I can go from being a super stressed-out and insecure little girl to being a lead actress in feature films and TV, and speaking on stage in front of thousands, then so can you. I'm no different from you.

I still have that little girl in me, but every day, I have the choice. Am I going to give in to that fear? Or am I going to step into my faith and my power, into the possibility, and use what I like to call "the disruption muscle." I can disrupt the way I perceive something so that, rather than disempowering me, it empowers me to take action. All I have to focus on is, "What am I doing today to get me one step closer? What am I going to create today? How can I see this day, this experience, as a creative process that I'm participating in? I'm not just going through the motions – I'm co-creating my reality."

There's so much power deep inside you. I hope, from the bottom of my heart, that you hear this message and KNOW you matter. I hope you know that you are more than enough. You are capable of doing amazing things. You have the power to disrupt doubt, and fear, and limiting beliefs, every single day. You have the power to co-create the life of your dreams.

Choose to be the hero of your own life.

It's a gift.

Choice is the best gift we have.

Keep choosing to be brave. End that toxic relationship. Make that hard phone call. Keep going even if you're afraid.
— Rachele Brooke Smith

CHAPTER FOUR

~

Putting a Spotlight on the Gaslighter

by Amy J. Morrison
Founder, Empower Her Power
www.linktr.ee/AmyMorrison.EmpowerHerPower

It was as if Satan was staring at me. The look on his face said, "It took you long enough." My hands were holding on tight to his shirt, and my only thought was, "He's going down the stairs."

I heard this voice inside of my head and it had different plans. It was God saying, "You'll be the one going to jail. Let go."

It's usually subtle, but what they do is like the fable describing a frog in boiling water being slowly boiled alive. The premise is that if a frog is put suddenly into boiling water, it will jump out. If the frog is put in tepid water, which is then brought to a boil slowly, it will not perceive the danger and will be cooked to death.

This is the narcissist personality, the gaslighter, the person who appears to be very nice and caring when, in actuality, they are conniving and manipulative.

"Oh, that'll never happen to me," is what most women say. But it can happen right under your nose. And you won't have any idea what's going on because you love him, he's the best thing that's ever happened to you, he loves you, he's got your best interest at heart.

When it dawned on me that I was standing there contemplating, I wondered, "How did I get to this place? I'm not like this. This isn't my personality. I'm a good person."

Our relationship started off great. We were in love. He was so kind and gentle and he doted on me. We spent a lot of time together and then got married. Our daughter being born was one of the happiest days of my life.

He bought me things and took good care of me. He even bought my clothes. As he was taking care of me, what I hadn't realized was he actually was controlling me to the point that I became decision-less.

I learned not too long ago that when we first got married, he drove to my mom's house without me knowing and told her that she couldn't buy clothes for me for Christmas anymore because it was his "job." He controlled people around me without me knowing. He controlled my friends and my family, not just me. So I completely shut down.

After being told for five years that I was crazy, I stopped talking. Truth is, I was telling myself I was crazy. He never said that. That's the thing about gaslighting, you start to question your own sanity because of the manipulation thrust upon you on a daily basis. Any time I would bring up something, a confrontation would occur and it would always end up being my fault.

A gaslighter has a knack for preying on a person's insecurities. They know exactly what to say and do to make you feel like they are there to help you, to save you from your life. Things like, "Oh, your parents didn't do that for you? I'll do that," are words they use to make it sound as if you were neglected by your friends and family and that they are there to give you what you want and deserve. This is to get you into their clutches and to start trusting them. They use a very clever form of manipulation that leads you into questioning your own sanity.

When they're feeling down, it's your "job" to make them happy so you can get back to the honeymoon phase and everything will be okay.

Gaslighting isn't limited to only spouses, but also to friends, kids, family, co-workers; it's an epidemic. And it's not going away anytime soon.

Knowing the signs that you're being gaslighted and then having the courage to admit that it's happening to you (that was the hardest part, realizing that I allowed this to happen to me) will help you step out of it and move on with your life.

For several years my sanity was being tested BIG TIME. The person I loved and trusted was manipulating me into believing that I was absolutely bat shit crazy, making me question my reality.

Because of your trust in them, you don't question their behavior. You believe it's YOU who is messed up. You know they would never do anything to harm you because they love you so much.

Unfortunately, it doesn't work that way. While anyone is susceptible to gaslighting, knowing the signs can help you come to your senses and get out before you believe you're going insane. You may not believe you're being brainwashed, so listen to people who tell you you are. They just may be right.

Here are a few tell-tale signs that you're being gaslighted:

They tell blatant lies.

You know they're telling a lie and so do they. They're setting you up to question their every move. This slowly leads to you questioning your every move. Doubt starts to set in. They're trying to get you off balance, and it's working.

Denial of what they said.

You have proof that they said something, but they flat-out deny it. Again, you start questioning yourself. "Did they really say what I think they said? Did I make it up?" You start accepting their lie as the truth.

They use your family and friends against you.

They attack your relationships with others. They give you reason to doubt your friendships and relationships. They attack and you start to believe them.

The daunting wear-down.

Gaslighting is a long game tactic, one that takes cold, harsh, manipulative games to get you to believe you are crazy. Because of this, even the brightest minds on the planet are susceptible to falling prey to it. They'll start with a small white lie or two, then move into a mean remark here and there, and then, once they have you in their clenches, they start picking up speed because they know they have you.

Monkey see, monkey do.

Not with a gaslighter. Their words don't match their actions. Pay more attention to what they do than what they say.

Massive confusion coming your way.

Hmmmmm, they've spent so much time putting you down, but now they're complimenting you? What's going on? It's in their plan. They know you're starting to question their putting you down, so they throw in a compliment here and there. They're trying to get you to believe that they're not so bad because, after all, they're saying nice things about you. Most likely the compliment was actually something that benefits them and not you.

Pitting your loved ones against you.

They tell those you love that you're crazy. This tactic is dismissive, and they know that if they question your sanity, your family and friends will never believe you when you tell them the gaslighter is abusive or out-of-control because "you're the crazy one, not them."

If you know someone who uses these tactics against you, the first thing to do is to admit it's happening. It's real. You're NOT crazy. They're manipulating you. Remember, even the most brilliant people on the planet can be manipulated by these people. Most of them have been doing this their whole life, so they're masters at their craft.

One night I was praying to God for Him to give my husband the wife he needs and praying for me to be the mom my children needs. I was done, wasn't good enough, and was a burden. I didn't want to be alive anymore.

It was the next morning when my three-year-old daughter put her hands on my face and said, "Mommy, I'm happy you're alive," that I knew I had to do something.

Sometimes it takes a wake-up call for us to know it's time to do something different in our life. God had to use a 2x4 to get me out and wake me up. You don't have to wait that long.

If you see any of the above signs, ask for help. Find someone you can turn to who will be there for you. I found The Landmark Forum. It has helped me tremendously.

The psychological abuse is one that can last forever unless we get help. While I've made a lot of progress, the damage is locked inside my head and I'm pulling it out of there a little bit at a time. I'm still working on getting better and developing trust in myself and others.

It's an ongoing battle inside my head that I'm winning.

CHAPTER FIVE

~

Your Life Is Yours

by Angelica Waruguru Waite
Owner, Advantage Eco Trails and Events
http://advantagecotrails.co.ke

I was the youngest of nine children, in a prayerful Catholic family. As it often is with siblings, I took the blame for most things, but the truth was that my home was filled with lots of love. Still, as the baby in the herd, I often felt invisible amongst all the chaos of a big family.

I discovered that I craved the spotlight, so I learned to sing. I wanted to be out in front, singing solos, and that's what I did. Later, in 1985, when I attended college, I discovered within me a deep drive to lead. While studying tourism, I led the Catholic Action Group and my drive increased. One thing I didn't do was date, which is a thing most women do in college- explore their options. I was raised to believe that dating equals marriage, and since I wasn't ready for that, I simply avoided the whole thing.

After college, I started working and dating a man. Because of the way I was raised, I didn't really comprehend that I could make choices and date other men. So I married him.

Marriage to my husband was the complete opposite of the way it was in my family. Not only was he a terrible provider, but he expected me to provide for him. To say this was shocking is an understatement. I realized I was trapped in this marriage with two kids and no support. I was married-single. I felt unsafe, unprotected, like I was drowning and there was no hope of rescue.

I had no choice but to step up into the leadership role in the family. The rent had to be paid and the kids had to be fed, so I did whatever it took. I landed a job as a travel consultant and did odd jobs on the side. I turned my car into a little shop and sold secondhand clothes and fleece blankets and other things out of the trunk. I saved the extra money from my side biz and eventually built a home for me and my family. My husband did have one redeeming quality: he was great with our kids. He took care of them while I worked, made sure they got to school, and was just generally a really good dad. As long as I was paying the bills, things went smoothly.

It was good that I could trust him with our children because I was working myself to the bones to grow my travel consultant career. And I was good. I moved up to a managerial position. Clients loved me, and I developed good relationships with my co-workers. I had manifested my desire to lead into becoming the sole support of a family of four.

In 1998, when my younger child was two years old, my husband asked me for 100,000 shillings. He said he had a business opportunity and was going to be out of the country for a while. He took the money and disappeared. I never once heard from him. I had no idea if he was dead or alive, or if he had just used this mysterious "business opportunity" as an excuse to run out on us.

This was so painful for me that I began to contemplate suicide. I was trapped in a dark place. I couldn't move. I couldn't breathe. I thought I had failed as a wife and mother.

One day, I met a client for tea. She listened while the story spilled out of me. She said something to me that day that hit me right in the gut: "Your life is yours, Angie. No one else's. What do you want to do with it?"

She was right! Regardless of what my husband did, I knew I had the right stuff to make life work for me and my kids. And that's when I knew I could not only survive – I could thrive.

I made the choice to live. I decided to change so much that my husband wouldn't recognize me… if he ever came back. And I stopped worrying about whether he would come back or not. I was the provider for my kids. I didn't need him.

He did come back… three months later. He never offered any explanations. He just walked in one day and expected that we would just welcome him back… and that I would continue to support him.

And I did. My Catholic upbringing was strong in me, and I couldn't face the idea of divorce. I hung in there, despite my unhappiness. To this day, I feel the effects of this experience. For example: I always overshop when I buy groceries. It's like I need to know that I'm well-supplied just in case he pulls the rug out from under my life again. I still grapple with that fear of losing everything.

Then, one day in 2016, disaster struck. I had just returned from leave, taking care of my daughter and new grandbaby. My boss asked me to meet him at the cafeteria near the office. This was not unusual. The entire office staff typically had meetings there.

But this time was different. I walked in with a notebook and pen to find the entire management team there. Gulp. What was wrong?

I sat in horror as they accused me of starting my own agency behind their backs and stealing their clients.

"That is not true," I protested. "Ask any client if I ever solicited them. I never did."

As they discussed, my mind drifted to how much I had put into this company, working long hours without extra compensation, including consistently going beyond the call of duty.

No matter what I said, they refused to acknowledge that I had once again performed above and beyond my responsibilities. I couldn't believe this. If I were guilty, I could have easily paid my own agency.

There would be no investigation, only accusation. They escorted me to my office, made me box up my personal things, and tossed me out on the street, empty-handed after 17 years of total dedication.

How could this happen? How could I lose it all when I had done everything right? The sense of loss and fear nearly overpowered me. I sat on a curb, holding my box and thinking, "I can go home and cry or I can move on. Whatever I do, the bills will still come."

So, I packed up my car and drove around looking for office space. All I could find was a table at a Java coffeeshop. I started calling my clients. And then I did what I had been accused of- I "stole" their clients. Nearly every client went with me because they admired my work ethic and knew I was the best. Some of them said they only worked with my company because I was there.

Ironic, isn't it? Had my employers believed me, they would have kept their clients.

Too bad for them.

Eight days later, I found a small office space, moved in, sat on the floor, and finally allowed myself to cry. I needed that release of emotion for my own sanity. When the tears stopped, I picked myself up and said, "I will make it."

Determined as I was, the journey was challenging. It took grit and determination, but I built my travel tourism business into a solid one.

Then, in 2020, Covid hit, and boom. The entire travel business dried up overnight. I had no choice but to re-center myself again. I thought, "I know I can sell, so what can I find to sell?" I hustled to sell fleece blankets and fancy hats with built-in masks out of my car. I fed my family in spite of whatever drama was going on around me.

What has come from this lifetime of struggle? My kids and I have a solid relationship. My daughter has a Master's degree, two beautiful children, and works with me in eco-tourism. She is growing her own brand as a sustainability consultant. My son is an architect. I am beyond proud of them.

I tell women who are considering starting their own businesses, "The right time to start is now. Now is what you got." I learned to make quick decisions – no more hemming and hawing over details. I love myself now. It is the most wonderful feeling to bless others and help them get on their way to loving and respecting themselves as well.

If I could say one thing to women everywhere, it would be this,

Women, stand strong. Your life is yours. Be invincible.
— **Angelica Waruguru Waite**

CHAPTER SIX

❧

The Magic of Surrender

by Betty Morin
Experiential Speaker, Yoga & Meditation
Coach and Human BEing
www.MoveInwardUplift.com

"You were diagnosed at 11 with manic depression. Do you agree with that diagnosis?"

In our initial consultation my therapist asked me this question. I sat dumbfounded on the toilet (don't worry - we were on the phone). I had no idea how to answer.

"I don't know," I said, confused but resolute.

"Maybe something to explore in the coming weeks," she said.

So I did. I read the Diagnostic and Statistical Manual of Mental Disorders (DSM) IV under which I was diagnosed in the mid-1990s. I looked it up in the DSM V, under which "manic depression" was moved to a category of bipolar. I took it all in and looked at the diagnosis head on. After reading an article on highly functioning people with severe mental illness I realized, "This is my experience."

Once I surrendered and was able to name it, everything shifted, and magic began to appear. I saw the "rollercoaster" of my life: tumultuous relationships, high highs, deep lows, inexplicable mood swings, deep fear, bursts of creative energy gone just as quickly as they came. I suddenly had the opportunity to see with "new" eyes that I was not living in choice, but rather at the mercy of mental illness. In that moment I experienced freedom.

I have amassed many tools over the years. In May 2009, my mother gave me the gift of learning Ascension meditation taught by the Ishayas of the Bright Path. This gentle meditation practice uses simple techniques that allow me to rest in the infinite stillness within. At first I believed it wouldn't work and practiced to prove my point. However, there was magic almost immediately and the only thing different was Ascension. I noticed the deep, crippling fear was dissolving. My life had an underlying sense of peace that I had not experienced since I was a child.

In the Fall of 2011, just one month after getting married, I attended Yoga Teacher Training. Here I began a healing process with my body. I am only now, years later, blossoming into this healing and infinite love that I am experiencing, but that's another story entirely.

My Ascension practice gives me the space to observe thoughts, and to choose what to pick up and what I do not need (spoiler: I'm finding I don't *need* any of them). Movement allows me the space to experience my body, practice self-love and detach from thought on a physical level.

But these practices alone were not enough. The diagnosis kept coming up - one minute there was peace, pure presence, unyielding JOY, and the next, I could be on the floor, heaving tears for no apparent reason, living in fear.

In 2020, my life took an unexpected turn. I joined the team of a nonprofit after being largely out of the workforce since the birth of my first child in 2014. This nonprofit acts as a bridge between mental health providers and those who need them. Here I had an opportunity, a safety, to see what this diagnosis was doing in my life.

My husband and I began to fight. It was the same fight we've had so many times about nothing and everything questioning why we even love each other because we're SO different; leaving us disempowered, disconnected, and sad. This fight lasted for almost two weeks - a record for us - and I realized something *had* to change. He was willing to go to couples therapy as was I, though we never got there due to COVID-19. But his willingness shifted something for me and I found my therapist.

Now we come full circle to that probing, poignant question that changed everything! At our first tele-health visit, my therapist and I spoke about the diagnosis of bipolar again, and we decided I needed a prescribing psychiatrist to help me create a medication plan. It took me almost two weeks to start looking; I was terrified. Terrified of the cost, side effects of the drugs, you name it, I was afraid. I called a trusted friend and colleague who offered resources, and I was able to contact a provider. Her $500 consultation fee scared me, too - more fear, more "proof" that this was insurmountable.

So, I did what any self-respecting woman in this day and age does and I took to Facebook. Here is an excerpt from my post from June 23, 2020:

Posting here to say, I am not okay today.
I was diagnosed with manic depression when I was 11.
I have largely ignored this diagnosis. But now, seeing it, naming it, allows me to be objective. So, I'm looking at it, I am empowered and hopeful as I look.
I feel strongly about using this platform as a place to share fully and honestly. I share my children with you, I share family time, I share my deeply held views on

equity, peace, love. I share a lot and it wouldn't be honest
to not share this.

If you, too, are moving through the waters of a mental
health journey, you are not alone. It's okay to not be okay,
and when you're there know I am here for you.

In this public surrender I felt seen and loved. Friends commented,
reached out, told me I was brave, people I'm not close to private-mes-
saged me. Magic occurred when a dear friend who I knew from yoga
school reminded me that she is a seasoned board-certified psychiatrist
and offered to help me through the medication plan on this journey!
No $500 consultation fee to meet with a stranger, instead talking to a
friend who I know loves me. I jumped at the opportunity. In a 20-min-
ute phone call, we had a plan which she emailed to me so I could move
forward with my physician.

The doctor I normally see couldn't meet with me soon enough so
I opted to meet with his PA: more surrender, more magic. My doctor's
PA is originally from Taiwan, a mother of two boys, a kind, loving person. She and I hit it off instantly, and she spent over an hour with me in
that first appointment. We went through my whole history; I showed
her the detailed medication plan. She agreed that it was perfect, en-
sured I had a therapist, and instructed me to come back in two weeks
to follow up. That was it, easy.

I began taking the mood stabilizer along with the anti-anxiety
medication I was already on and a myriad of other vitamins and supplements I ingest daily. I felt a shift. Whether this was all in my head
or not, I don't care - something was shifting. It took months for me to
surrender to the therapeutic dose I needed but I was now rarely afraid
of turning into the Incredible Hulk, and then hiding under a rock a
split second later. I was experiencing myself more; the person who has
so much joy inside that she might explode!

At this same time in my life I was larger physically than I had ever been; I felt yucky in my own skin. I struggled with an unhealthy relationship with food, seeing it as an enemy. And I had a belief that I was not disciplined and everything I commit to I quit, especially anything to do with physical health.

In July 2020, I went to visit my sister, taking my two boys (six and three at the time) to visit their cousins. She and I spoke briefly about the Whole30 and maybe doing it when I got back to Utah. I looked through her recipe book and chose some dishes that made my mouth water and filed it away for "one day." When I got back to Utah, she texted me on a Friday asking if I wanted to start on Monday. I said, "Nope. But I will." More surrender, more magic.

My commitment to my health was showing up, I had chosen to treat the undulations of my mood, I was now going into a new way of eating, I was seeing a therapist, and was playing in the waters of surrender. The diagnosis I had been walking around with, like a chain around my ankles, was broken, and I was living in choice. The pieces were all coming together and all it took was one question, a little action, and surrendering the outcome for the magic to work.

The universe, God, source, has my back - has your back. It takes commitment to be present, to trust, to say, "Yes, I'll have more of that, please, or better." This is my experience.

And so, my friend, I invite you to find your tools to surrender. Surrender from the space of trust, not defeat. The Truth is flexible, malleable, the Truth wants us to find it - it shows up in religion, spiritual practices, our bodies, friendships, asking for help, and in being vulnerable. It is EVERYWHERE and we have only to surrender to it and allow the magic.

CHAPTER SEVEN

~

You Are Not the Sum of What Others Think of You

by Bridgetti Lim Banda
Executive Producer, BLive Media
www.BLiveMedia.com

I will never forget the look on my dad's face as he made the last choice left to him. December 17, 2021, marks the third year since my dad closed his eyes for the last time in my arms. It's been three years of gut-wrenching turmoil in my head trying to make sense of a life that was, that is, and will never be the same again. The final memories with my dad will be with me forever.

Over the years, I have watched many loved ones and friends take their last breath and I supported the ones they left behind. Most notably were an aunt, an uncle, my grandmother, and my mother and father-in-law. Those impactful moments will forever be etched in my mind and hold a special place in my heart. Each moment I've had the privilege of witnessing loved ones take their final breath was extraordinary for different reasons. Somehow having my dad, the man that gave me life, look at me in a way that is almost indescribable as he took his final gasp of air and then closed his eyes for the last time left me breathless and speechless.

Reflecting on my life, in a weird way, feels like poetic justice because I was never good enough, or so I believed. Over the years, I carried with me many labels, and one of the most significant was not being good enough. Not a good enough child, daughter, student, wife or even mother. In fact, I was not good enough to the point of being labeled stupid by those in my life. Stupid was probably the label that was the hardest to live with but also the one that finally helped set me free.

Ironically, I was the one who was "stupid" enough to know that my dad had reached a point of no return in his journey as a stroke survivor. I knew it was just a matter of time. I remember the day I received the call to say that something was wrong with my dad, and despite what our relationship had been like, I just knew I had to do the right thing and go to him. I was shocked to discover that my dad had slowly been starving because he couldn't swallow. I asked for a feeding tube to be inserted and the doctor didn't argue. It wasn't exactly a happy moment because nothing about death and dying brings happiness. Still, it was one of those moments that made me feel like I wasn't stupid after all.

The weeks and days leading up to that moment when my dad closed his eyes and took his last breath in my arms were heart-wrenching. The sibling rivalry, the fights with caregivers, the fights with my mother all because I was the "stupid one" who knew nothing. Yet, I was the only one who was "smart" enough to know that the time had come to make some tough decisions about my dad. And I knew that leaving my dad's side was not an option.

Leaving behind my own family responsibilities and the comfort of my bed (which was my refuge because I am a chronic pain sufferer) didn't matter because I had a singular focus of supporting my dad in his final hours of his life. I was there for many others, but it had become an obsession for me to be there for my father. For weeks I pushed through my body's pain barriers and gave up my sleep because I wanted to do all I could for the man who gave me life. It was all worth it, and I have no regrets. I may not have been the perfect daughter, but I finally got to hear my dad say he loved me for the first time before he died. From that moment, nothing else mattered, and when he closed his eyes in my arms, I was numb, sad, and overcome with grief.

What I didn't feel for the first time in a long while was stupid. From that moment onwards I decided that it no longer mattered what others thought of me and that it was time to unpack the rucksack of rocks I had been carrying all my life. I needed to learn to quiet down those voices in my head.

I got an opportunity to do this after another life-changing event. I had to have neck surgery and still had a long way to go in my recovery journey, but I knew something in my life had to change. I decided that livestreaming was going to be that change. I believed that I could make a difference, and so without much training and only an inner belief that I was good enough, I went live on air. The first time I went live on air with newly released third party livestreaming software, I was unfortunately knocked down by a narcissist who told me to move over because I wasn't good enough. Another voice I had to squash.

With a sense of determination, I moved forward and found a cause I could get behind. The timing could not have been more perfect. The Cape Town water crisis was starting to emerge in South Africa. I realized that livestreaming could give me a unique opportunity to create a platform to share unfiltered and unbiased news, information, and education. This was the fuel to push me through the attack on my self-esteem. I decided that I was not going to let the voice of an online bully derail me from my plans or interfere with delivering a service to my community.

I knew nothing about water other than just being a consumer. Still, I also knew that I could share information with my audience if I could surround myself with knowledgeable and respected experts in the water industry. I was truly humbled by the experts I approached that freely shared their expertise. Before long, I became a trusted voice for the Cape Town water crisis with the information and help I received from these water professionals, and I am very grateful to them. I was interviewed several times on national and international radio and television. I was quoted in numerous articles and even had a part in an international miniseries about the water crisis. BLive Media provided a platform and was a significant part in connecting water professionals with the public who might otherwise not have had a voice during that critical time. This is how I launched my career as a remote Livestream Producer and Talk Show Host.

I have grown to love livestreaming. I enjoy the connections, friendships, and the unlikely friendships I have made. The online bully I mentioned before coincidentally connected me to a group of six amazing women from around the globe. Even though we live on different continents and time-zones, livestreaming connected us and forged lasting relationships. It was from one of these friendships that The Writers Corner Live TV Show was born. We started the show on a whim, and almost three years later, we have done over 133 episodes and interviewed world-famous authors from around the globe, and the show is still going strong.

Livestreaming has not only connected me to people I might never have met and built friendships with, but it also taught me that almost anything is possible. My voice matters: I am not stupid. It was time for my mantra to change, and I am forever grateful.

With my newfound confidence I set my sights on livestreaming on the worlds' largest business platform. When the LinkedIn Live Beta program rolled out, I bravely applied and stated that I wanted to become the first livestreamer in Africa to gain access to this exclusive network. On June 9, 2019, I was able to check this off my bucket list. Imagine that being an insignificant unknown person in my little corner of the globe, and I had convinced LinkedIn, the largest business platform in the world, to let me livestream on their platform and be able to share information and knowledge to a global audience, and I was the first person in Africa to do so.

I was also a group moderator with Be.Live TV for four years with a network of 27,000 people. I could never imagine having that kind of influence and impact had it not been for livestreaming. I'm presently a group moderator with Streamyard who was recently swooped up by the Hopin Network, which has given it a substantial global representation in the livestreaming community.

I am beyond thrilled to have been a part of the livestreaming community's growth and journey. I am thankful for the friendships and impact I've been able to make along the way. It has not only given me the freedom and confidence to broadcast to a global audience, but it's also given me the confidence to feel worthy, and I have been able to teach and pass on my skills to many others. For the first time, I truly feel invisible no more. Someone else's narrative doesn't have to be my truth anymore.

CHAPTER EIGHT

~

Peek-a-Boo! I Don't See You!

by Cathy Derksen
Transformational Success Coach,
Inspired Tenacity
www.InspiredTenacity.com

How many times have you played this game with a small child? You know, the one where you disappear every time you cover your face and reappear every time you reveal yourself again. This game brings on fits of laughter from the child as you disappear and reappear. It makes me giggle just remembering playing it with children.

Unfortunately, thinking of this game also makes me realize that this was how I have lived many parts of my life: disappear, reappear, disappear, reappear....... In my case, instead of fits of laughter, I was experiencing alternating success with phases of loneliness, frustration and depression. There were many times when I felt invisible. I now look back on those days and appreciate how far I have come.

During childhood, my family moved several times. Each time was another awkward restart. At times I felt invisible, and other times I wished I were invisible to escape the bullies that were intent on finding the newcomers. In high school I was fortunate enough to have a few teachers that really connected with me and helped me to see a whole new world of possibility. I began excelling at almost everything I took on. I had opportunities fall in my lap as I took on every challenge that came my way.

Through most of my 20s I was shining. I looked to the future with excitement and anticipation. I did all of the things that were "expected" of me: graduated university, built a great career, married, bought a house, started a family. My inner light was shining brightly.

Unfortunately, my light began to fade as I moved through my 30s. I experienced postpartum depression as a new mother and life became overwhelming. As the stress of parenthood set in, my marriage crumbled under the pressure. My husband, who had been excited with our new life, shifted into an abusive, angry person who took his frustration out on me and the kids. Over the years I felt my identity fading away. I was losing myself in my role as a mother and wife. I found myself putting aside all of my dreams and desires in order to keep the peace at home.

I had become invisible once again. In life's game of Peek-a-Boo, I had disappeared.

For years I allowed myself to take the back seat and to put everyone's needs ahead of my own. Our family dynamics became increasingly toxic and volatile. As my children moved through their teens, they both handled the stress in their own way, becoming withdrawn and self destructive, or lashing out trying to stand up to the abuse. Our family had become a bomb ready to explode.

In a situation like this, it often takes a major shock to jolt us out of the dark hole. Roughly 10 years ago my family was involved in a tragic car accident. We were physically unharmed, but will be forever traumatized by witnessing the horrific death of the fellow on the motorbike that T-boned our vehicle at high speed. This shocking event sent us each into our own unique way of coping with the shock and trauma. This became the life event that woke me up to the reality we had been living in. I woke up to the realization that I needed to lead my family out of the mess we were in. It was at that time that I found the strength to rise up and push aside the darkness that had been hanging over me for so many years.

This awakening was followed by many challenging events. By the time the dust had settled I had created a new life for myself and my children. I left the abusive marriage that had defined me for so long. I moved my kids into a new home where we could begin to create a life built on positive goals moving forward. In this process of awakening and reinventing my life I realized that the job I had been in for many years was also very toxic, filled with immature politics and bullying. I made the decision to correct that aspect of my life as well and set out on an entirely new career path.

Throughout this process of shifting my life, there were many times that I wanted to turn back to the comfort of familiar times. There were many times when people told me I was crazy. Sometimes I thought the same myself. I was determined and focused on the new life I was creating. There were nights when I cried myself to sleep under the pressure of carrying my family through this huge transition. There were times that I questioned my ability to take on a whole new career in my mid-40s. I created a mantra that kept me focused. "Chin up, keep moving" was a phrase I said to myself over and over. Sometimes quietly in my mind. "Chin up, keep moving," sometimes out loud. "Chin Up! Keep moving!" Sometimes I would scream it in my head just to keep myself from turning back when things got really tough. "Chin UP!! Keep MOVING!!"

This was when I made the decision that I would not allow myself to be invisible ever again. I would not allow myself to disregard my needs to keep the peace. I would not allow others to belittle and abuse me ever again. This was my time to step up and follow my passion.

I know I am not alone in my story and I know that many women disregard their own needs to the point that our physical and mental health suffer. I have made it my mission to be a shining light for the women of my community. We can be invincible when we look after ourselves and look out for each other. As I moved forward in this evolution, I felt called to share the lessons I've learned with my community. No more disappearing in the lifelong game of Peek-a-Boo.

Over the past year I have developed an online community focused on creating a safe, supportive, inspiring, motivating, inclusive place for women to come together. As women we often lose track of our own goals as we get busy in life as mothers, caretakers and dedicated employees and business owners. When you feel that life is drifting past, it's time to take a leap of faith and create a life that brings you joy. Allow yourself to shine! Give yourself permission to think about yourself and where you want the next chapter of your life to lead. Will you go back to school, start a new business, discover new hobbies, spend more time with friends or traveling? Will you leave a toxic marriage or workplace? I'm not suggesting that we should just walk away from our problems, but if you have done your best to correct a situation and there has been no positive change, sometimes you have to move yourself in another direction. Allow yourself to dream again! Through the programs I run I feel a great sense of excitement as I witness women creating a life that allows them to shine.

My mission is to create a community of success and wealth among women. It has been my experience that, when women experience support that allows them to create positive change in their life, they naturally want to help others do the same. As I assist in women creating success in their own life, I trust they will step up and help others do the same. Recent news reports tell us that women should plan to live into their 80s and 90s. We have gained extensive experience and wisdom over the years. Let's apply these talents to bring LIFE to our life. Whether you are in your 40s or into your 70s, you have many more chapters to write in your story.

Step out of your current comfort zone and give yourself permission to live a life that makes you feel excited to get out of bed every morning. Push away the guilt and fear that hold you back from taking a leap of faith toward your dreams. So many of us are living with feelings of frustration and longing like there is something missing. Life is not about going through the motions everyday just to make it to the next day. Life is about contributing in a way that inspires and motivates you. I have named my online community 'Inspired Tenacity' as I feel this is what we need to make big changes. We need to be inspired by following our heart and we need the tenacity to push past the nay-sayers and obstacles in our way.

If you feel that you are living life feeling stagnant and invisible, connect with the women around you for support and encouragement. The online world has brought us all closer together. By leaning into our dreams and leaning on each other for support, we can shift from invisible to INVINCIBLE.

~

CHAPTER NINE

Love Yourself So Others Can Love You; Be Kind to Yourself So Others Can Be Kind to You

by Cecilia Rankin
Health & Life Coach, Health Coaching 4ever
https://chooseyourpathwithcecyourcoach.now.site

Now that I am 52 years old, with a wonderful husband and a successful 25-year-old son, I can say, "Life is good." For a few years in my life that wasn't the case.

A Child's Lament

"Don't judge a parent until you know their story."

My life began in Vietnam before the Vietnam War started. I remember my dad owning a restaurant. I still have fond memories of hopping onto the bar stool and him making a bowl of rice slide down the table for me to catch. My job, at the restaurant, was to hold the door open for people to enter. I remember my mother taking me to the beach and me laughing as she played tag with me.

The day my mother took me to an orphanage I did not know what was going on and had no idea that would be the last time I would see her. For the first few days, in the orphanage, I would cry and cry until I fell asleep. I remember a man, dressed as an American soldier, coming to visit me. I didn't recognize him as my father because he looked so different with a uniform on. I was hesitant to go to him until he pulled out a piece of candy for me to take. He gave me an orange flavored Pixie Stix. Once I tasted that candy, orange became my favorite flavor! Being at the orphanage was not bad. There were other children to play with. I remember us playing with our shadows. We pretended to be in a band and would line up to watch our shadows move on the brick building.

There are just two scary moments I have of the orphanage. The first one was when the Communist soldiers came marching into the orphanage with their rifles. The sight and sound of them marching on the cobblestone scared me so much that I hid inside of a locker. The other scary memory I have was at nighttime. The girls slept in one room and the boys slept in the room next to us. During stormy nights water would creep down the wall and the building felt shaky when thunder and lightning cracked the air. Lucky for me I was on the bottom bunk and under my bed there was a small hole that went to the boys' room. There, next to the boys' room, was the laundry room where the nuns could be heard talking as they did the laundry. On stormy nights I would crawl under my bed, crawl through the hole, and sleep under one of the boy's bunk to have the comfort of a light shining with voices nearby.

I don't know how long I was in the orphanage, but I do remember when a nun took me out. I held her hand as she walked me over to another building. We climbed up some steps and in a room another lady was waiting for us. There the nun left me. Once again, I cried uncontrollably. The stranger put pajamas on me and set me in a crib. She left and closed the door behind her. She left me alone screaming and crying. The crib was by a big window where I could look out. I saw a nun sitting on a park bench. Lucky for me the window was open. I climbed up onto the windowsill and decided that I would fly over to her. The next memory was in the hospital. I must have landed in some bushes because I did not break any bones.

My final day in Vietnam I was taken to a school bus. Waiting there was the strange looking soldier who once gave me the orange candy. He was dressed in an American soldier uniform looking so dashing. He gave me a hug and put me on the school bus. I ran to the back of the bus to wave at him. As I waved at him, I saw him crying. Once again, I started to cry, but this time silently to myself. That would be the last time I would ever see my father.

Another Life In A Strange World

"Being a parent is tough, but being a child is tougher."

Unbeknownst to me, the day I got onto the school bus, I was headed to America where I would be adopted. To this day I don't know how old I am. In the Vietnamese culture, at least back then, people did not celebrate birthdays. I still wonder if my birth parents truly didn't know my age or if they made me younger so I would be more adoptable. My passport said I was two years old. Now, as an adult, I do not agree with that because I have too many memories of Vietnam and my parents.

At the airport there was a tall, white man waiting for me. He had white hair, white suit, and white shoes. Thinking back on him, he looked like Colonel Fried Chicken. I don't remember much of the flight but I do remember meeting the family that was supposed to adopt me at the airport.

My new family had five children of their own. I had two sisters about the same age as me and three older brothers. One would think that a large family would be a happy one. It was nothing of the sort. The turmoil of my childhood would cause me to become invisible. The family severely physically, sexually, verbally, and emotionally abused me. I don't remember what happened but I was put in a foster home and then sent back to the family where they continued to starve and beat me. During my stay with them, the only comfort I had was dreaming about my birth parents and longing to be back with them. At night I would quietly cry myself to sleep and just imagine myself in a happy home.

With this abusive family I had to be hospitalized three times before I was finally taken out of the home. I started out living in a hospital where I loved the nurses. One nurse spent a lot of time with me and she even took me out to play at a park. I loved her so much that I wished I could live with her. The day I was put into a foster home she took me there. I remember sitting on the steps with her feeling so sad. I always wondered if I had told her, I wanted her to adopt me if she would have taken me. I was too scared and shy to tell her. The only thing I did was hold back my tears and just waited for nighttime to come for me to silently let out my sorrow.

There is one foster family that I have fond memories of. There were at least two teenage kids in that family. I loved being with them because they loved me and we had so much fun playing at their cabin. I don't remember how long I was with them but I enjoyed every minute with them. Whenever a foster family went on a trip out of state, I was not allowed to go with them. Sad to say, the fun foster family had to leave me behind with someone else. I went to three different foster homes before I was finally adopted.

My Final Move

"To heal, one must forgive without forgetting."

I was finally going to be adopted by a family. According to my passport, I was seven years old. My brother was six. He, too, was adopted. He is African-American and was born in the United States. He was adopted when he was a baby. I loved being with my brother. He was (and still is) gregarious and a fun person to be around. Both of my parents had siblings. My father had six siblings and my mother had four. We tended to be closer to my father's side because his parents lived just two hours away from us. I loved all of my aunts, uncles and cousins. I have fond memories of family get togethers and trips with my cousins.

From the outside, our family appeared happy and normal. But, behind closed doors, there was grief. I do not want to get into details about the hardships I experienced with them. I am happy that I was given another opportunity to live and have a somewhat normal childhood. We went to church and took part in the youth group. My parents were active in our church and community. Life with my new family was good most of the time. In my adulthood I realized there was no family that did not have struggles. I was always amazed at couples who I thought had the "perfect happy life" ended up divorcing because they, too, had challenges.

When I was in high school, I would daydream about my future. I dreamed of creating an orphanage where children could feel loved and safe. My other dream was to have at least seven kids to have a house full of fun and laughter. One most important dream was to be happy and enjoy my adulthood. The first two dreams never happened, but the latter did.

Becoming Invincible

"Choice determines your destiny" ~ Aristotle

Once I graduated from high school I went away for college. That first year was not a good one for me. I had too much fun and did not take my education seriously and got into marijuana. I was majoring in business only because my parents wanted me to. In my heart I knew that was not what I wanted. I had wanted to be a pediatrician to help children. Due to my low self-esteem, I did not feel like I was smart enough to be a doctor. During my time off of school I had three jobs to be able to live on my own. During that time, I met my husband. He was so in love with me that I wondered why and how anyone could love me that much. From my traumatic childhood I made a promise to myself that I would not marry a guy until I knew he came from a good family. One test I had, for a guy, was how quickly he introduced me to his family and friends. Another test was how well he treated his mother. How a man treats and talks to his parents, especially his mother, says a lot about his character. Well, he passed the test!

Once I decided to settle down with Steve, I decided to go back to college to get my teaching degree. I was able to finish my four year degree in three years! Once I graduated from college and found a teaching job we got married.

The day my son was born I marveled at how perfect and peaceful he looked. My little boy became my treasure and the best gift I could've asked for. Sometimes while he slept, I would just stare at him and wonder about how difficult it would be for a parent to give up their child. At what age can a child be taken from you before he forgot his birth parents? It made me realize that I was fortunate enough to be able to remember my birth parents.

Somehow I was able to take the correct path to help me find happiness as an adult. Now I am a teacher and a health/life coach. As a health and life coach I have a passion to help others love their bodies and find happiness in life. As an elementary teacher I want to give hope and support to children who struggle. I want all of the girls, especially immigrant girls, to be strong and let them know there is hope once they become an adult. Nothing, not even the virus, can stop me from giving children hugs when they need one. How one speaks to a child can make a difference in his or her life.

When my son was about eleven years old, as I was tucking him in bed, he hugged me and said, "Mama, when I climb the Seven Summits, I'm going to climb Everest last. You know why?" "Why, sweetie?" I asked. "Because when I climb it, you will be dead and then if I die on Everest, I won't care because I'll know you're in heaven and I will get to be there with you." That night I cried with happiness, instead of sorrow, knowing that I had done my job of raising a loving and caring child.

For those who have difficulties overcoming their past, just remember there is hope if you are willing to open up and share your story. Talking about your struggles can help you heal. Everyone has a story to tell and as humans we love listening to them.

I would like to give thanks to Lynda for giving me the opportunity to tell my story!

"Life is full of field trips; take as many as you can before life passes by."

~

CHAPTER TEN

Finding the Light at the End of the Tunnel

by Dr. Christine Sauer
Founder, DocChristine Coaching
https://DocChristine.com

2 0 years ago, my life ended. I was driving back from Bayer's Lake to Halifax, on the 102 highway.

I was sitting in my burgundy van, feeling the worst in my whole life.

My body felt numb from physical pain and my mind was enshrouded by dark, painful, seemingly impenetrable clouds.

I felt completely and hopelessly stuck in the darkest place of my life.

I pushed the gas pedal down as far as it would go, took off my seatbelt, and picked the bridge pillar on the right side of the highway that looked sturdy enough to hold up to a deadly collision.

I was ready to die. I still remember this moment as if it was today, and I shudder thinking of it.

Obviously, I didn't do it, or I wouldn't be here today.

What happened?

Just two years earlier, I was working 14-hour days in my large der-
matology and naturopathic office in Germany, trying to help as many
patients as possible in the short amount of time – on average 5 to 10
minutes – the German health system allotted to them.

After work I was coming home, only to work some more in my
ex-husband's family practice, participate in nightshifts, house calls,
weekends and holidays, as well as doing emergency duty.

I had no time for myself, for my own health, and was feeling more
and more frustrated, stressed-out and burnt-out.

Something had to give, and for me, it was my back.

One day it started. A sharp pain went through my back as I sat
down on my office chair.

I didn't think much of it and continued to work away.

On the evening of this day, I could hardly tie my shoes…but I drove
home and went straight to bed.

The next morning, when I woke up, I couldn't move. The pain was
excruciating. My ex-husband called his ambulance-friends and I was
carried down the stairs and put in hospital. I stayed there for 4 weeks,
learning to walk again.

I must say, the experience of not only switching roles and being a
patient, but being completely helpless and bedridden, thankfully just
for a week, and dependent on others for the basic functions of life, and
yes, I mean peeing and pooping while laying in bed – was extremely
humbling, embarrassing and devastating.

I stayed hopeful through all this, and entered a rehab program,
slowly re-building my strength.

I decided to sell half of my practice to a partner.

After some time I started working again, first part-time, then slowly building up.

And – boom – it hit me again – another disc slipped and I was back in bed again, in renewed agony, physically and emotionally.

This time I gave up. I felt hopeless, stuck, trapped, and felt my life was over.

I decided to sell the rest of my practice and fell into a deep depression.

And for me, I had learned in my childhood to soothe emotional pain by eating, preferably sweets. And believe me, German cake is delicious…

I was rudderless, not knowing what to do with myself and where to go in my life.

Shortly after that, my ex-husband decided to commit suicide and I was left sick, with two teenage boys – and immigration papers to Canada.

You see, 3 years before that, we had started immigration procedures as we didn't want our boys to have to serve in the then-compulsory German army.

Life takes strange turns sometimes – and so I decided to come to Halifax, Nova Scotia.

It was a turning point for good in my life, although at first it seemed to make things worse.

Isolated, without friends or family except two spoiled, demanding, and unsupportive teenage boys, in physical and emotional pain, I felt stuck in a dark tunnel with no end in sight.

That's when I took my van and wanted to end it all.

So - what was it that stopped me?

As I was heading for the bridge post, I heard a small, tiny inner voice in my gut telling me:

"Christine, you don't want to die, you want help! You have things to do with your life!"

I am very grateful I listened to this inner voice, and with tears of desperation streaming down my face, and feeling like a failure – I couldn't even kill myself – I headed for the emergency room.

I was very fortunate that the resident who saw me recognized the seriousness of my situation and admitted me to the mental hospital, where I spent 4 weeks listening to John Denver music, waiting for the medication to kick in. It did after a while, and after another 6 weeks in the outpatient day treatment program I was ready to continue the struggle on my own.

And a struggle it was. I still was in the dark part of the tunnel.

To really understand the tunnel metaphor, you need to know that in the European mountains, where the more-than-a-mile-long tunnels are, the tunnels are not straight, but have a bend at the end to avoid the drivers being blinded by the bright light at the end. When you drive into one of such tunnels, you see only the darkness at first.

But then, a sudden turn at the end, and the glaze of the southern sun brightens your spirit. As a child, we drove through tunnels like that many times.

Little did I know then that life has those sudden turns, too.

For me, the turning point was making the decision to change. Not to accept the downhill spiral I was in.

The decision to get back to doing what I was passionate about all my life, which is and always was helping other people with their health and lives.

I always have been a researcher, loved to read, learn new things, study and apply this knowledge to help my patients.

Now I also had a chock full of life experience to offer....

But what could I do here in Canada? I pondered going back to Germany, but I had found the love of my life here in Halifax, and my dear husband was not suited at all for German life.

I decided to search for options to fulfill my destiny here at my new home.

I had tried to get a license to practice here, took the tests required and passed them, but couldn't do the residency they demanded because of my illnesses. Now it was too late.

I tried different things, studied business administration, became an expert tax preparer, but these I couldn't feel passionate about as much as I tried. I am passionate about people, not money...

I finally took several health and life coaching programs and other courses related to my true passion.

And now I am living my passion for helping people with their own health and helping them honor their struggles as I honored and still honor my own.

After adjusting my own lifestyle, nutrition and supplements as well as working on my thought patterns, I am now happier than ever and barreling forward to the end of helping as many people as I can afford to.

We all are on a learning and growing path and I learned that this is ok. It truly is NEVER TOO LATE to live your best life!

"If you are stuck in a dark place, I want to tell you: Don't Give Up! There's a light at the end of the tunnel for you, too! (and it's not a freight train)."

CHAPTER ELEVEN

~

The Shroud of Shame

by Delores Garcia
Founder, Delores Garcia Coaching
https://deloresgarciacoaching.now.site

I remember leaning over and peering into his casket. My older brother was holding me in his arms so I could see. I was all of 4 years old. As we stood at the open casket, my mom looked me in the eyes and told me to tell my dad "Good Night, Daddy."

He had ended his life a week prior.

And thus began my journey as an invisible girl. My father's suicide became a huge dirty secret that I shamefully kept hidden from the world, lugging it from place to place. It grew into a thick shroud of disabling shame, burying me within.

It was a cruel task master for such a little girl.

I almost let the cat out of the bag in 7th Grade Science class. I remember it so clearly. A classmate was pestering me about not having a dad. I told him that he died. It was the truth. The boy asked how he died. I told him he got shot. It was the truth. He was astonished. He then asked if they knew who did it. Yes, they knew. It was the truth. The teacher then interrupted the interrogation. It was all just a dirty little secret filled with wretched shame that I could do nothing about. Just shove it down a little further and continue pretending you are normal, as the shameful secret continues to whisper messages to the contrary.

I wonder what would have happened if I had told that boy the whole truth.

Life went on the best it could, I suppose, but my experiences as an invisible little girl continued within the family also. I understand now how my mom was nearly broken, merely surviving, after having nine children with my alcoholic narcissistic father. I was the ninth child in this sea of children. Mom passed away when I was 33. When we were at her viewing, many of the people who came to pay their last respects could not comprehend who I was by my name; they needed to know what "number" I was. It seemed to symbolize my life: what place value did your life have. No identity . . . just take a number. And it seemed I carried the brunt of the shame of having "so many" (aka too many) children that she could barely take care of. I carried the shameful responsibility of being #9 of too many children. Just like I carried the shame of my father's suicide.

Shame at every turn. And the shroud thickened.

We attended church every Sunday. This could have been a balm of healing, but sadly it wasn't. I wanted to be a good Christian, worthy of God's approval. But, instead, I felt destitute of hope for redemption. I sung the Sunday School songs with the rest of the children about being "children of God," although I highly doubted that I personally was divinely created like everyone else. I can clearly see myself as a small girl in the chapel, singing that song, and actually looking around at the other children, thinking, "You all are children of God, but me? No, not me. I am just extra parts that they threw together. There is nothing divine about me." Remember, I was a mistake. I had dirty secrets. I was so full of shame. I didn't know how to feel divine; I only knew how to feel

ashamed of my very existence. That is what shame incessantly whispers
. . . you should be ashamed of yourself . . . you are a mistake . . . you are
breathing too much air and taking up too much space . . . stay small.

I could not reconcile this pain as a child.

It was no surprise I struggled with depression. It is very difficult to
be positive and optimistic when you feel ashamed of your very essence,
your very existence. I actually accomplished a lot with my life, but each
seemed a frail attempt to add a drop of value to my pitiful existence.
The underlying code of self-loathing prevented me from feeling happy
and enjoying life. I actually had a loving husband, two beautiful children, a custom home on country property. Two playful dogs in the
backyard. I was a college professor. It was a dream life on the exterior.
But the depression continued to plague me. I was still searching for
happiness. Always searching.

And yet, not even knowing what I was searching for. What was
missing?

I honor myself for staying on that endless quest. Could I ever be
happy, truly happy? I kept searching, studying, counseling. I do not
discredit any of the books I read or the therapists I worked with . . .
it was an evolutionary process. It was my last therapist who cracked
the code of my 30-year depression. I laughed aloud when she told me
that depression wasn't really my problem. I thought, "No, lady, really!
Depression is a big problem. Haven't you been listening to me? You
should be inside the darkness with me." She proposed that I was so low
in self-esteem and that that would be where the healing needed to happen. I initially dismissed the idea, but it remained in my heart. I knew
I hated myself and my very existence. But that wasn't really a diagnosis,
was it? Depression was a <u>real</u> diagnosis and that's what I had always
clung to. And, yet, getting to the root of the outward symptom is where
the power of healing is. I began that journey, healing the relationship

with myself, progressively transforming from absolute self-loathing, eventually to soulful self-love. I continue that journey today.

The Shroud of Shame completely obscured Me from Myself. **I** was what I was missing. I was invisible even to myself.

As I shift out of shame, I now practice a 'Life of Invincibility' which is me embracing my 'Dreams of Possibility.' I give myself permission to see myself and also to be seen. Whenever I hear myself say "I always wanted to . . . ," I face the fears, take the risks, and get to living that dream. Like writing books. I always wanted to write a book when I was a little girl. And here you are reading my story! Invincible! Or having a strong, sexy body. I entered a physique / bodybuilding competition at the wonderful age of 52. Invincible! It is truly never too late. I now have a successful coaching business in which I guide my clients to their own healing so they can relish their own Invincibility. Living the dream!

Be very clear! None of the dreams I accomplish change my inherent value. I always was a Divine Creation. And always will be. And now that I know that, I function from that place instead of trying to create or prove my value with more accomplishments. I get to enjoy them like never before! From this place of self-love, I can then freely share my divine gifts. I am no longer lost!

Invisibility and Invincibility are perceptions. Feeling invisible was my attempt to cope with what happened in my young life. It doesn't matter what my story is, how it compares to another's tragedy, or how my siblings experienced the events. I learned to be invisible and continued living underneath that Shroud of Shame for nearly 50 years. It doesn't matter what your story is, what the events were, big or small. What matters is how you experienced them and how you have seen them play out in your life. Don't compare your story to another's. Honor your own struggle and your own path of learning. I share my story to honor my path. I honor you in your journey. Don't minimize your story, your experiences, or your pain. Take courage from these stories that you, too, can find answers to your personal questions, revealing your own Life of Invincibility. It is waiting for you!

It has been 50 years since my father's suicide - I turned 54 this year. I am writing this story while sitting in the park, watching two little towheaded girls play in the sprinklers. Coincidentally, they are 4 years old. I laugh-cry as I watch them squeal with delight in the freedom of innocence. As it should be. I see myself in them. Even so, I woke this morning with a little voice whispering old, recycled doubts that maybe I should not tell this story. The voice suggested that I should keep my business to myself, that it wasn't that big of a deal, that maybe I should just keep it safely buried. And then The Universe sent me those two little blondie girls to remind me of my Invincibility, to lovingly encourage me to write the story and leave it here for whomever. Let the light of the new day burn out the hideous secrets of yesterday. It is time to F.L.Y. ("First, Love Yourself.") It is time to be Invincible Forever More.

CHAPTER TWELVE

~

Imagine. Just Imagine: A Tribute to Emma Adams

Written by Delores Garcia

Emma was born in the springtime of 1927, the sixth child of Annie and Robert. Southern Idaho, with its dairies, corn and sugar beet farms, was a quilted patchwork in the fertile soil. This was the sixth home birth for Annie. That was life for them. But, wait! Imagine it. There was no Labor and Delivery at a sterilized hospital. There were no certified midwives. There were just the neighbors, sisters, older daughters attending. They had on-the-job training from their own birthing experiences. Just imagine!

A short 14 years later (and 5 more children), Annie transitioned to her next life. Her passing left Emma as the oldest daughter at home, who now was expected to mother the five younger siblings. 1941. Emma continued to go to school, a definitive privilege for country girls. She would knead the bread dough before going to school. It would rise during the day. And she would bake when she returned from school. Laundry by hand. Out houses. Weekly baths with shared water that had been warmed on the stove. The girls would have to wash their "rags" out by hand that they used to absorb their menstrual bleeding. Imagine. Just imagine. Walking to and from town, school, church. Home gardening. Milking the cows. Sacrificing the chickens and plucking feathers. This was life.

As an inescapable expectation and perhaps as a tribute to the mother she adored, the young girlie rose up to meet her newly assigned life. That's how all the girls were referred to by their father: "girlie." Names were just a legality, not an identity, to him. Imagine. Even when I knew him as the very old man as my grandfather, he continued that tradition. All females were called "girlie." Just imagine. He never bothered himself to know their name. Wonder if Annie, his wife, was called "Annie" or "sweetheart" or just "girlie"?

On her own deathbed, Emma revealed a deep, dark secret. As a beautiful young lady, with a sparkle in her clear emerald green eyes, she would go to the social dances that the soldiers attended. One night she was enticed outside of the dance hall and deceptively taken to the dark shadows. And it happened. She would never be able to admit her "sin" to anyone. She was a good little Mormon girl from pioneer stock. And now she was the substitute matriarch of the family. And she had sinned by being raped. The secret, the shame, the unforgivable sin was forever hers to bear alone. Imagine! With no one to help her carry this burden, she buried it into the depth of her soul. The depth of the shame matched the weight of this tremendous burden. The utter inability to be forgiven by God. The utter impossibility to forgive herself, feeling fundamentally unworthy at her very core. She had spoiled the sacred goods of being a woman.

What was a girl to do? No mother. A father who did not acknowledge her humanity, let alone her innocence and divine worth. An ultra-strict religion with a punitive moral code with absolute zero tolerance for sexual impurity. Suffocating societal devaluation of women.

Imagine. Emma had been sinful in her beauty, in seducing the soldier, in smiling too pretty, in making the soldier lose control of himself. She really was just too pretty in that dress. She did this to herself. She brought it on herself. It was her fault. And it was now her sin to bear alone. She was truly on her own now. Just imagine.

So she buried it. And she continued on with her assigned lot in life, mothering her younger siblings. Then she met Bill. This charismatic ex-Navyman promised her a new life. She dropped out of high school and they hitchhiked from Southern Idaho to his hometown. Imagine. Just Imagine. 1943. They married soon after arriving in Houston. Their first child was born the next year, the year she turned 17.

But life really didn't feel much different than when she was back home in Idaho.

I am the last of the nine children born to Emma and Bill. Because I was barely four when he committed suicide, I was spared the abuse and heartache. And, in many ways, I had the best of my mother. The alcoholic narcissist was finally physically gone, although deep wounds remained. Imagine recovering from your alcoholic narcissistic husband's suicide with five kids still to raise! Nevertheless, my childhood really was an average childhood with less-than-average dramas.

In reflection, I now see the true invincibility of my mother. Although she did not finish high school, she taught me such academic confidence that I not only finished high school, but then junior college, then undergraduate, and then graduate school. What she taught me eventually led me to a professorship at the university. I credit my test-taking skills and academic confidence to my "under-educated, high school drop out" mom. We would bring our class notes to her and she would decipher them on the spot and spontaneously formulate questions to prepare us for exams. It seemed like magic! How did she even know what questions to ask?! And that was the skill she taught me

. . . how to anticipate the questions so you can have the answers prepared. Imagine. I clearly see this connection to my career as a professor.

Although she was on government assistance when Bill abandoned her with the six older kids, I never lived in government housing or was on food stamps. The point of this observation is not to judge Americans who are on assistance. The point is that this girlie-with-no-name from small town Idaho single-handedly raised nine children without a high school education, in spite of an alcoholic narcissistic man coming in and out of her life. Deeply burying the immense pain of losing her angel mother so young, intermingled with the hideous shame of being raped, she quietly taught me invincibility. We lived in good houses, good neighborhoods, and had what we needed. Just imagine.

A rich part of Mom's invincibility was that she covertly taught me to dream and aspire. I was not crippled by her personal experiences and paradigms of invisibility. Despite this legacy of invincibility, I do feel like Mom died still feeling invisible. I feel sad about that. Her indomitable will to just keep going is the example of invincibility that I grew up with. Yes, there were times that she didn't support me the way I had wished she had and I have processed through those painful emotions in my own spiritual journey. Ironically, one of the things I did not feel supported about was my writing. Funny, huh?! I remember I had written a story. Excitedly read it to her. And got an absolutely flat response. Ugh. But here I am, authoring my first published works in my mid-fifties! And writing about her! Imagine. It's never too late to achieve your dreams, with or without support. You just keep going. Because you are invincible.

When I was starting first grade, I heard the family talking about Mom passing her GED. I didn't really know what that was, but I remember it seemed like a big deal. Formal education was a matter of opportunity, not a matter of intelligence, for her. She was one of the most intelligent, quick thinkers I have yet to meet. Yet she never made me feel less-than. It was more like she made me feel like I had received the greatest endowment of intelligence from her side of the genetic code. I never questioned my capability to learn what I needed to learn in school, even if it was challenging like calculus or biochemistry. You just keep going.

Mom was invincible in her absolute self-sacrifice for her children. While I resented not getting absolutely everything I wanted as a child (aka diva teenager), I now see the sacrifices Mom made for her children, to the bitter end, as a profound part of her indomitable invincibility. You just could not stop this woman. She had a job to do. And she was committed to doing it. I do, however, believe her physical body was ravished with many health conditions, spiking during my early college days, from her buried emotional traumas. She was in ICU one particular time for 3 months. Imagine. And yet she still came home and continued onward for many more years. Just imagine.

How I wish Mom could have truly lived IN her invincibility, that she could have enjoyed that empowered identity. I wish that for all of us. Life is messy, chaotic, riddled with challenges. It is not always pretty. But that feeling of invincibility carries us through these trenches. And so I write this tribute with the pure intent to proclaim this from the mountaintops . . . Emma IS Invincible Forevermore. And so it is.

CHAPTER THIRTEEN

Ghost

by Kristy Boyd Johnson
Boss Lady, Turtle Sea Books
www.TurtleSeaBooks.com

Creativity - like human life itself - begins in darkness.
— Julia Cameron

"Goddamn snotnose kids shouldn't be seen or heard," my father would scream at me for the vile crime of – gasp – walking into a room. "Goddamn kids ruin your life."

Yep, I was quite the little hooligan – fingerpainting, reading, watching TV. When would the madness stop?

Wait a sec. Hold on.

I could share my story, tell you all the gory details, but you know what? It's yet another story of yet another abused child who – surprise! – made a lot of mistakes as she dealt with all her inner demons. You've heard it all before, and I don't want to bore you.

What I really want to say is that none of that matters. What really matters is how we use our life experiences to grow, change, and create a good life full of love and friendships. I can't tell you what to do, but I can share a few of the significant things I did to transform my life.

Because I was so emotionally abused, the biggest demon that haunted me was the Shyness Dragon. Even now, I admit, I still struggle with this one quite a bit. Shyness comes from insecurity and a lack of self-worth. It's tough to develop self-worth when you are told how worthless you are every minute of every day. Shyness caused me all kinds of problems over the years, including during the writing of this chapter. I almost didn't do it.

But here goes.

I learned to write early in my twenties. I started writing stories in college and carried that skill into my teaching career. I would make up goofy stories for my kiddoes, and they liked those more than the books on my shelves. I kept learning, worked at improving my craft.

But, at age 25, I made THE biggest mistake of my life – I got married to a predator who thought he could use my Shyness Dragon to keep me under his thumb and in indentured servitude to his every whim.

Thus began the Coma Years.

For eight nightmarish years, I was lost. I take that back – for seven years I was lost. The eighth year was a year of awakening for me, and reconnecting with my inner Viking warrior woman. And boy, did she come out, sword swinging.

Unfortunately, my renewed spirit and smart mouth caused an escalation of the abuse. I spent many a night locked in the bathroom.

One fine day, I ran. I know beyond all doubt that, had I stayed, I would literally not be alive today. But it had taken me those eight years to get to a place of fearlessness within myself, to an inner place of Light where he could not, and dared not, follow me. And running into the Light felt really good, like I was escaping a vampire.

I spent the next two years trying to get a divorce, without letting him find me. That entire time, I was euphorically happy, even though I was practically destitute. I worked my ass off, re-connected with friends, and just generally enjoyed the peacefulness of living without fear of being punched in the face.

To supplement teaching, I began ghostwriting, and discovered I was good at it. Non-fiction is a whole different animal than fiction, and frankly, much easier. I used ghostwriting to supplement my abysmal teaching income while also working hard to give my clients a unique voice.

But writing is a solitary pursuit and did not trigger the Shyness Dragon to come out and play. Yet I knew it was still there, lying in slumber, just biding its time. Even a party invitation could freak me out. Better to stay home with a hot cup of cocoa, a great book, and my cat purring on my lap.

One day, on a whim, I walked into a Toastmasters meeting and joined the club. Something was awake in me, something urging me to get out there.

In Toastmasters, everyone is required to do an icebreaker speech, which breaks the ice with the group as well as breaking your personal ice on your first speech.

And oh, was my first speech bad. And when I say bad, I mean terrible. Awful. Depressing. Totally sucky.

"How bad?" you ask. Let me tell you.

Bad #1: it was boring as hell – a self-indulgent recitation of a traumatic injury that happened when I was sixteen.

Really, Kristy?

Bad #2: my knees quaked so badly that nearly every comment was, "You were shaking."

Yeah. Thanks. I hadn't noticed.

Bad #3: I cried. Real tears, running down my cheeks. I couldn't help it and couldn't stop it. And they weren't authentic tears from sharing a deeply heartfelt story, oh no. They were the "I'm having a breakdown on the stage" kind that makes one feel like diving into a vat of Valium, and, in the case of one (me) who was attempting to slay the Shyness Dragon, head for the beach and swim out into the vast open ocean, sharks and currents be damned.

But, the Toastmasters, oh, they were gracious. And kind. And lovely. And wonderful. With their love and support, I came back. And I did better on the next speech, and the next, and kept on improving under their guidance, kind comments, and indomitable spirit.

Let me just say, if you want to learn public speaking, go to Toastmasters. They completely rock.

The next thing I did was join an Improv comedy class. I wanted to be able to riff with the audience rather than just memorize my lines. I really admired the seasoned speakers who were able to do that with such ease and confidence and humor.

Improv is a place where the cool kids (aka: nerds. Our respective nerd statuses were discussed. A lot.) let go of all their daily stresses and romp with the other cool kids. The Shyness Dragon retreated a bit during this time, and I began to learn what it was like to relax and enjoy the company of warm, fun, non-judgmental people. Plus, every game, every experience, helped to skyrocket my skills into the stratosphere, and soon I was applying the skills to my speeches.

After some serious nagging… I mean, *encouragement,* my mentor signed me up for a contest. And boom. The Dragon awoke and roared.

But you know what? I did it. And even more freaky – I won.

Back in the real world, I expanded from ghostwriting into editing because, yes, I am one of those obnoxious know-it-alls who mentally corrects grammar, spelling, and punctuation errors. (But not out loud. I'm not *that* insufferable.) Why not get paid for it?

Later, I expanded again, but into book coaching, and that was when I found myself falling into a groove. Coaching allowed me to guide an aspiring author into finding their own authentic voice, rather than me trying to capture it. It's empowering for my clients and a lot more fun for me.

Fast forward to today, with the whole world in flux, including me.

I'm figuring out how to create group classes that are fresh and different from every other writing class out there. I want to do that in conjunction with writing retreats that will give aspiring writers both creative inspiration and concrete, practical advice while also allowing me to satisfy my own wanderlust.

I find joy in empowering my writing clients rather than taking over for them. They get to feel the immense satisfaction that comes from writing, completing, and publishing a book – their own book.

Best of all, my business partner and I are now producing Micro-eBooks for clients. These are short fiction or non-fiction books of 10,000 words or fewer and can be used in so many amazing ways: lead magnets, supplemental materials like workbooks, coloring books, children's books, journals – pretty much whatever you can imagine.

It's fun for us, and exciting for our clients who don't have to assassinate their budgets in order to create amazing materials to ramp up their businesses.

In all honesty, I haven't slain the Shyness Dragon. The best I can claim is that it's lulled to sleep and a spirit of adventure has awakened. When it comes to this, it's one day at a time.

I can live with that.

The road to hell is paved with adverbs.
— Stephen King

CHAPTER FOURTEEN

~

Thriving After the Sinister Hand of My Father, the Pedophile

by Krysten Maracle
Founder, Maracle Mastermind
https:Facebook.com/krysten.maracle

As an incest survivor for approximately 10 years, it took me a long time to talk about my abusive childhood and the sick, dysfunctional family that raised me. In this chapter I hope to help someone who feels silenced or "invisible" by suffering such unjust sexual abuse or any injustices to eventually feeling powerful, confident and "invincible" forever more.

My upbringing appeared very "vogue" on the outside. I grew up in a prestigious, upper class neighborhood ("The Wooded Area in Point Loma") in San Diego, California. My parents were members of the San Diego Yacht Club owning a large Yacht and drove a modest station wagon or a classic Cadillac with bat wings. Every summer was spent at Catalina Island having fun in the sun: swimming, fishing, diving, and water skiing. This may seem like a very charmed life, but it was not.

My life was horrific living with my father, who is a pedophile, grooming me from a very young age (probably 3 or 4 years old) until I was 13 years old. As a child, it was hard to understand the sick, seductive and creepy affection my dad showered on me when we were alone.

My mother would yell at me, "Get out of our bed, and go to your room!" I would cry at night wondering why she would not protect me from him. I could not understand why she would not ask me if I was Ok. What was happening under those covers? She had to know something evil was transpiring. Why would she yell at me? Perplexed as to why my mother never questioned my father; why did she yell at me and not my father? He was the abuser, not me!

None of this made sense to me. As a result, I retreated inward, silenced and afraid, feeling invisible and not loved by either parent. I did not have the courage to talk to anyone. I did not want to be judged by others. I did not want people to think I was "damaged goods." I wanted people to believe I was whole and pristine, not damaged and dirty. All the thoughts came rushing through my head: "Who could I trust enough to talk about this private matter?" "Who would believe me?" "What could my trusted agent do anyway?"

I finally realized that I was stuck in this abusive family, both passively and aggressively, because I had nowhere else to escape. So that is exactly what I did… feeling invisible, going thru the motions to survive these traumatic days, which progressed into traumatic weeks, which later turned into traumatic years!

My Mom, "Mrs. Denial," ignored any signs of abuse since she was dependent on my father as a Homemaker. Since my father controlled the purse strings, all of us (my brother, mother, and I) were victims to my powerful, sick, wealthy father's mental, physical and verbal abuse as well. No one stood up to my father because you would be physically hit and verbally shamed. The consequences were too extreme to utter a word. I remember saying to myself when I was around 10 years old that I would never marry a rich man because I felt he would control my life with no escape.

My parents divorced when I was 13 and my only sibling (my brother Bryce) was 15 years old. Unfortunately, I felt guilty and ashamed of their separation since I internalized the divorce and thought it was my fault by assuming that I was the one interfering with my mother's and father's relationship. This was a heavy burden for a child my age to carry on my shoulders. Within one year, my mother married a man that she dated in high school. I was SHOCKED when my mother told us that we were moving from the only house I'd known my entire life in California to Pennsylvania!

What? Leaving all my friends from Dana Junior High School?

No Long-distance phone calls? What!?

No... There must be a mistake! It can't be true! MOVING to PENNSYLVANIA?!

Where is that even on a map????

My world turned upside down socially and I was devastated, crying a river of tears.

That night I looked at the bright side which outweighed everything. I was elated to escape the hands of my father! I will be FREE from the abuse and tyranny!

Praise the Lord!
Hallelujah!
A new beginning!
A time to Heal!
A time to Soar!
A time to be Me!

Unfortunately, moving across the country was not as wonderful and easy as I had dreamed. I had more challenges ahead and another serious "blow" to my self-esteem. After taking the entrance exam for my new school, Swarthmore High School, I was told I was dyslexic due to my difficulty with reading and did not score adequately on the exams. As a result, I was held back a grade and had to repeat the 8th grade. This news was devasting. What am I going to tell my parents? What are people going to think? Good thing no one knows me here. Oh boy, yet another secret to hide! My new friends did not need to know about my biological pedophile father nor my repeating the 8th grade. After all, I did not want people to think that I was both scarred and stupid.

In order for me to feel good about myself, I decided that the entrance exam test result was not going to determine my future nor define me. As a result, for the first time, I made academics a priority in my life receiving honor society every year from 8th to 12th grade while playing varsity sports in tennis, basketball and track. It felt good to "prove the authorities wrong." I knew I could do well if I applied myself at school. I was excited to attend college because I wanted to be financially independent.

After attending Allegheny College for 3 years, I transferred to San Diego State University (SDSU) because I missed my community, beaches and great weather. I obtained my Bachelor's degree in Computer Science in 1987 as a member of Upsilon Pi Epsilon (UPE) Honor Society. I retired after 30+ years from Space and Naval Warfare Systems Center, Pacific (SSC-PACIFIC) in the Cyber Security Department, now known as Navy Information Warfare Center (NWIC) located in Point Loma where I grew up as a child. You might say that my life had come "full circle."

Unfortunately, during my Civilian career, when I was 35 and my brother was 37, I got the phone call from my Mom that my only sibling, Bryce, died of suicide at her house. Once again, the pain and shame bubbled up. My mind started swirling "I was not there for him," "What more could I have done," "Why did he not call me?" My "survivor's guilt" was in full-swing.

Even worse, I came to find out that my pedophile father had victimized many more young children. As a result, he was even forced to leave the San Diego Yacht Club or else charges would have been filed. Now "guilt by association" was in full-swing even though I had nothing to do with any of his crimes.

Through these horrific events, I have found that speaking the truth and being visible about my life as well as finding forgiveness for those that have hurt me is where I discovered my power and self-confidence. I am "Invisible No More; Invincible Forever More!"

This is the "real" key to personal freedom. One may ask, "How could you forgive your parents for their neglect and severe abuse?" I have forgiven my mother through much soul searching. However, I still struggle with forgiving my father for the long-lasting sexual, physical, emotional and verbal abuse that I endured. It has been a LONG process, well over 40 years. Everything takes time and it has not been easy. I keep a gratitude journal and studied many inspirational books. Most importantly, I am the daughter of the most high God. "For God so loved the world that he gave his one and only son, that whoever believes in him shall not perish but have eternal life." (John 3:16)

Jesus is my savior and I'm proud to be his precious daughter.

On June 4, 2020, I was interviewed on Season 1, Episode 6 by Mistie Layne on her "Dare 2 Share" show. For the first time, I publicly shared my background and story at the age of 56.

This was my BIG breakthrough. Breaking the SILENCE to the public.

It is written, "The truth shall set you free!" (John 8:32)

No more secrets! I am free indeed!

Below are a few books that I highly recommend:

"Jesus Calling" by Sarah Young

"Change Your Thoughts, Change our Life" by Dr. Wayne Dyer

"Ask and It Is Given" by Ester and Jerry Hicks

"Edgar Cayce Thoughts for the Day (365 Inspiring Lessons)" by Kieth VonderOhe

Always remember, it is not what one has been through, but, more importantly, where one is going!

Please do not allow abuse from the past or an exam define you. You are much greater and stronger than you realize. You were born to be YOU!

Please keep your joy and inner peace. Do not allow anyone to steal your joy and inner peace. Continue to look for Angels in your Life, they are everywhere.

I hope and pray that by sharing my experiences with you it has given you hope and inspiration to have a more purposeful and happier life.

Please join me in my Facebook group "Maracle 'LIVE' Mastermind," which is intended to give HOPE to others in honor of my late brother Bryce. Please feel free to contact me through Facebook messenger if you would like to connect or have any questions.

Stay Safe, Stay Healthy, and Stay Blessed.

Namaste!

Krysten Maracle

~

Building My Unique Invincibility: Invisible to Invincible Forever

by Krystylle Richardson
Founder/CEO Life Innovation,
Woman Weekend-Preneur
https://krystyllerichardson.com

Invisible, what a lonely word when it is attached to a living being.

I was hurt. I felt like that invisible person. I was totally consumed with wanting to be accepted by certain people in past relationships that I did what they did just to be a part of the group. It is disappointing how much time I wasted and we all waste on this type of behavior just to later find out that those people were a flash in our lives. At the time, I thought the world began and ended with those people. Not so. This made me invisible to them and to myself. Ignoring who you are just to fit in, makes you invisible to others and to yourself. I had to do something about how I was feeling. It did not serve me well. Being whole emotionally helps us to fulfill our dreams and reach our destiny. I am glad that I figured some things out before it was too late. It was time to start building my own unique invincibility.

As we move forward in this chapter I want to not just start writing for this chapter, but to, rather, have anyone reading take a moment to really ponder this word. Close your eyes and say the word 'invisible.' Think about any time in your life that you have felt this way. Think about any time in life when you have recognized that you have made someone else feel this way as well. Think about the time that you woke up to the fact that you either accidentally or purposefully walked past someone and then realized that they were there after the fact. Think about how you felt the time or times that this has happened to you. Stop. Think. What emotions come to mind? What good or uncomfortable feelings are in your mind and heart right now? Take at least 60 seconds to think on this. Are you done? Did you make it to 60 seconds? Now, as stated, before I start talking about my experiences and challenges related to this word, I want to have you do one more thing. Think about the homeless. When was the last time you saw a homeless person? Did you acknowledge them in any way? Did you walk past? Did you drive past? Did you make eye contact? Did you engage to determine what help they needed? Did you stop to think that your kindness and actions may either make them feel invisible or invincible in a way?

I hope this exercise was not too much for you. The point of it was to evoke some emotional ties to the two words by looking at them straight off the bat from 2 or 3 different vantage points. Let's go a bit further in this chapter and explore these two words. This type of exercise may have hit some of you very hard and may have been a bit uncomfortable. For others, it may have been a reflection of things already worked out and it was not so different to navigate the emotional ride. Whichever the case, I hope it at least got you thinking about these two powerful, powerful words: Invisible and Invincible.

The defining.

When I write in these types of chapters, I love to start out with a few personal definitions. For this one, invisible to me means to be a nothing in the eyes of everyone including myself. The word invincible means, to be in a state that has no words to describe it. The person or thing is so beyond unstoppable, beyond ending, beyond infinity, beyond confident, beyond actionable, beyond creative, beyond innovative, beyond fire, beyond supernatural, and beyond legacy. Invincible to me means something that I cannot fully explain. I will, though, take a crack at it, with my small contribution to this amazing collection of great thought leaders.

The dimensions of the seen and unseen.

You see, for years I lived in several different dimensions of the seen and unseen. In the dimension of the somewhat invisible in some areas of my life, to the out front let's "getter-done" mode in other areas of life. Part of the reason for the different dimensions was because of the effect of being bullied. I was bullied for many years, but 98% of the people in my life did not know this. I allowed a certain (un-named) personality type to control certain parts of my brain, actions and reactions. At first, I did not recognize that I was allowing myself to be manipulated in this way. It was not until I started deep prayer, fasting and self-evaluation that I was able to discern what was happening and what I was allowing. It is sad in some ways to think that this took me up to the age of 50 to figure out. I am glad, however, to know that I figured it out before age 100. That's good, right! (My attempt at a bit of humor.)

The point of it all.

I want to leave you with a few thoughts on how to stay in the realm of invincibility and be invisible no more based on my life. Here are a few tips on how to start building your own unique invincibility.

Invincible tip 1: Know when to start, stop and finish.

I feel most invincible when I set clear intentions and follow through. Sometimes things go as planned and sometimes they don't. That's ok. Do start. Don't talk yourself out of it because of what ifs. Be a finisher by setting intentions and holding yourself accountable or get an accountability partner.

TIP 1 FINAL THOUGHT: Be an invincible finisher.

Invincible tip 2: Be a person of forward adjustment and change.

Sometimes I do well with change and other times not so much. I have to keep telling myself that the change, no matter how large, some seemingly difficult, is a step towards being a better version of myself. Change happens so roll with it. Being open minded and creative on how to handle change when it happens is a good thing. Find a way to make change fun and lighthearted. Remember, no change means growth stops. Let's keep moving forward and grow.

TIP 2 FINAL THOUGHT: Be an invincible change agent.

Invincible tip 3: Pursue peace.

I love the calm and the refreshing that comes over me when I feel peaceful. It does no good for us to have all of these life pursuits and end up stressed, overtaxed mentally, physically exhausted and on edge day after day. Pursue the things that calm you daily. Have a quiet place physically or even a place you can go in your mind to bring you calm. Insist on keeping this time for yourself daily. This gives you the clear mind and power you need to fuel your dreams day after day. Do not miss this.

TIP 3 FINAL THOUGHT: Be at peace with being Invincible.

Invincible tip 4: Do the hard things.

I have pressed myself more these past 4 years than any other time in my life. It took doing hard things. Breaking out of being an introvert. Creating my own opportunities to build my circle. Meeting new people that were outside of my immediate circle. Being ok with operating on the edge of fear and potential disappointment on a constant basis. The interesting fact is, I would not change my journey for the world. It has come with tears from time to time but also resulting in strength. The life changes that come from doing hard things, makes it all worth it.

TIP 4 FINAL THOUGHT: Be the powerhouse that you are and embrace being Invincible.

Invincible tip 5: Stand even if you stand alone.

It has sometimes been hard to wrap my head around how much I have accomplished in my lifetime. It is always humbling when I get that little thank you note from people who appreciated me pouring into their life. Self-acceptance at any level is a good thing. The point of this tip, though, is to know that you cannot always take everyone with you, no matter how much you want to. Everyone does not want to play in your sandbox. If you have a burning desire in your mind and soul though, you must press forward even when it looks like the odds are against you. Don't give up. Remember to stand for right and stand for what you believe in. You will be a better and wiser person for it.

TIP 5 FINAL THOUGHT: Stand as an invincible force of nature who impacts nations.

I hope you gained some strength from this chapter. Let's be invincible together. Finally finding out and embracing that you are indeed truly invincible is freeing. Possibilities are endless. Impact can be greater. Monetary wealth can be no problem. Let's all discover and master our true freedom formulas and our Financial Independence Preparedness Plans (FIPP™) together. I love helping people through my Life Innovation initiatives to unleash their freedom formulas. I help people to get past mental barriers so they can discover the joy and freedom of life. In doing so, they discover untapped income they never knew they had. Money does not buy happiness. What it does do is it makes our time that God gave us on this earth easier to navigate as we pour into others, do you agree? Thank you for taking this journey with me. Let's consistently maintain a state of invincibility daily, are you with me? Let's go. Let's build.

CHAPTER SIXTEEN

~

Powerful Beyond Measure

by Legend Thurman
Doctor of Veterinary Medicine Candidate
www.Instagram.com/LegendThurman

My story begins like many others before me: I grew up in a small suburban town in south-western Pennsylvania with dreams that stretched beyond the borders of our county and the state line for that matter. However, my perceptions of the world, its inhabitants, and of myself were far from ideal. Constantly hearing the voice of Kelly Clarkson's song *Breakaway* ringing in my ears since its emergence in the early 2000s and the message it carried, the longing for more, the desire to make something of myself, and the strength to prove that I would not conform to the bonds of society had been activated. On the other hand, this eagerness was constricted by fear, one that was fueled by thoughts of inadequacy, anxiety, and imposter syndrome. My deepest fear was that I was damaged beyond repair, incapable of breaking the barriers placed before me until I realized that my deepest fear was not rooted in inferiority but, rather, of my own power within that was aching to surface.

I was raised by my great-aunt (whom I now refer to as my mom), her siblings, and her parents from about the age of five. They provided a safe and pleasant atmosphere to grow up in with my mom playing the role of both mother and father trying her best to block out the unpleasant times and overcome challenges as they presented themselves. My mom worked as an obstetrics and gynecology specialist nurse during the night so she would be able to take and pick me up from school every day. She and the rest of the family were always very supportive and encouraging in what I chose to do with my spare time amid my studies, but also pushed me to work hard since it was something that was always valued in one fashion or the other.

My birth parents were surprised with my arrival at a very young age and were not ready to accept the challenges of parenthood, nor do I blame them as they were only children themselves at the time. My father stayed around for a few years, but the bond that is usually created between a father and his daughter, unfortunately, was never formed. Instead, the few memories I have consist of him belittling my choices of after-school activities such as band instead of playing a sport, never showing up for parent-teacher conferences or performances, telling us he had been arrested for being involved in recreational drug sales, and my personal favorite: almost setting fire to our house with a joint. To be honest, I always felt like I was the daughter he received instead of the son he desperately wanted. However, the feelings of being under-valued never entered my mind at the time; instead, my trajectory was focused on my goals that were laid out before me to construct my long-term plan. Little did I know that I would carry these feelings into my adolescence and young adulthood.

Being from a small town also means you can live in an environment of narrow-minded people who think they have the right to infiltrate their beliefs upon you. All throughout my life, I have carried a fuller figure and while growing up people would love to push society's viewpoint upon me that if I did not look a certain way then it was wrong. I would be burdened with comments about how my self-image casted out a perception of what I had to offer to the world in terms of employment, finding a partner, or succeeding in life. Hearing phrases like "obese," "muffin-top," "panus stomach," or "she is never going to find someone looking how she does" would not only be taken as derogatory, but deplete my self-worth thinking that this image of what some people have labeled me with has now permanently defined who I am as a whole. Another factor was the idea of moving away from home. In the area where I was raised, a lot of people never left and, if you did, it was never looked upon favorably because you were defying the silent structure that seemed to be in place. There were times I did not have hope for humanity based on the personas that were illustrated; was there anything truly authentic that allowed someone to feel like they were a part of the bigger picture, accepted for every inch of their body, and loved down to the very core of their being? Or does everyone just settle for the habits that seem to have been set in stone and are practiced by those who are aiming to hurt?

Knowing I wanted to aspire to new heights, I moved to Washington, DC for college to attend the Catholic University of America where I would end up studying biology, chemistry, and theology/religious studies in preparation to apply to Veterinary School; I also got involved at the Basilica of the National Shrine of the Immaculate Conception. It was there that I built relationships with so many people that I now couldn't ever imagine life without. The Basilica truly gave me family members I never thought I would have who supported me along my journey through college and still do to this day. Unfortunately, during my time in DC, the self-image ideals that had been implanted in me were exacerbated further. I found myself in a relationship that demanded mental, emotional, and sexual abuse leaving me feeling like I had lost part of myself that I was working so hard to become in the long run. Why was it that again another individual seemed to not care or want anything to do with me no matter how hard I tried? Once again, instead, I pushed ahead thinking that if I can just get to veterinary school and exert every last ounce of energy I have, then things will eventually get better since I will have proven that I can make it and can accomplish anything I set my mind to.

Come January 2018, an offer from the Royal Veterinary College in London, England, the number one veterinary school in the world, found its way to me. So here I was packing up my life to move several thousand miles across the Atlantic, but there was one problem: I felt completely and utterly alone in the idea of who I was and possessed no grasp of how Legend Alexandra Thurman was going to fit into this status of a veterinarian let alone live up to the standards of this institution; imposter syndrome was sounding its alarm for sure. These factors skyrocketed my anxiety levels and as the first two years flew by, the attitude of feeling like I needed to prove myself remained intact. It was not until my third year that I experienced a shift in perspective, finally allowing me to gain clarity and eliminate that which was not serving me.

Consistently rooted in the idealism that I had to prove my worth to those around me, I had fallen into this trap of believing that my past, specific individual's opinions, and everyone else's agenda established my value and the basis of how I was to live my life. No, it's simply all about awareness. Charles Horton Cooley said it best: "I am not who I think I am; I am not who you think I am; I am who I think you think I am," proving the complex nature of the human identity based on the strictures of society. Through focus, commitment, repetition, and faith, I stepped into a new light recognizing that I, along with every single person in the world, is God's highest form of creation gifted with the ability to make decisions based on logic, feelings, and courage. Therefore, settling is an option but not a conscious choice. We have to think and act exactly like the person we want to become and that the simple choice of wanting to do so is all we need in order to succeed. The only person whose permission you need to break through the barriers standing in your way is yourself; you are the one you have been waiting for. Your authenticity and transparency is the seed that is planted in your core to leave your legacy.

It seems many individuals walk blindly through life thinking they need to hide their features, talents, and skills constantly worried about the perceptions of others. However, those opinions are only perspectives of judgments, not facts set in stone, and they are what hold so many people back. There are those who would question saying, "Who am I to be ....?" Well, let me ask you? Who are you not to be?! Labels do not equal permanence, and your purpose is power. The simple truth resonates in the essence of who we are. We are not invisible, but are truly invincible.

Putting these methods into practice, the new outlook I adapted for life required discipline, and I will not lie that there are good days and days that I still struggle greatly. Nevertheless, this vision of building my own platform has not been quiet. I now sit over in London working towards a Doctor of Veterinary Medicine degree with the intention of going into governmental work in the long run, something that definitely defies the norm. My purpose is rooted in that of servant leadership while being open to the possibility of change. Change is what we can count on since it provides chances of fulfillment; it is not something to be suspicious of. Therefore, I now choose to dare to lead with grit and grace that stems from the paradigm I now follow. My choice to liberate myself from my own fear and embrace every aspect of my being inside and out is the spark I am using to create my legacy.

Honestly, at the end of the day, we are the ones who live, die, and tell our stories. No one else receives that privilege except us. There are several quotes I live by, and one of them is *"Our Deepest Fear"* by Marianne Williamson, so I will leave you with my final thoughts inspired by Ms. Williamson. Do not fear the darkness or the light; for every piece of happiness, there is a foundation of unhappiness behind it that propels you to exactly where you are supposed to be. Trust yourself that you are worthy and that you are the very definition of love itself with the ability to let it shine onto others. And finally, you are powerful beyond measure with the capacity to make everlasting change that begins with you.

CHAPTER SEVENTEEN

~

There Are Times We All Wish We Were Invisible

by Mary Elizabeth Jackson
Owner, J5 Edutainment Inc
www.MaryEJackson.com

It is hard for us to truly be invisible because others physically see us on the outside. However, we can still feel unseen on the inside. Like being abandoned, ignored, or feeling invalidated by others. This can leave scars that stay with us forever. Feeling invisible sometimes never goes away when we accept it as a core belief about ourselves. As adults, we are motivated by our beliefs from childhood. It controls so much of us as we grow up and takes becoming aware of it in order to heal.

I was going to share about the time I was almost kidnapped, or the time my skirt fell off while I was performing on stage, but thought I'd save that for another time. These were both events where I truly wished I was invisible.

My parents divorced when I was around age ten-eleven. So I grew up with the experience of abandonment and that I was not important enough or good enough to be loved. Or so I thought because those were the messages I received.

When I was in junior high and going through that awkward stage, as most teens do, all I wanted to do was be invisible. I endured some scary bullying from some older kids, and it made it easier not to be seen even though I wanted to feel important or valuable. During the summer going into high school, some things changed a bit. I blossomed finally and started to feel visible and have dreams of what I wanted to do with my life. Dancing was a staple for me, and up until I was in my mid-twenties, singing, dancing, and theater were my big loves along with academics.

I got married at twenty-four. Around this time something happened with my health and my whole life and all of my dreams went in a different direction. They basically came to a halt. My life was filled with trying to find out what was happening to me–an internal belief manifested physically–that something was wrong with me. Why wasn't I good enough and so on. In a span of three to four years, I went from 115 pounds to almost 300 pounds. It was devastating. I was 24 and had been small my whole life. As a dancer, your body is your tool. Panic is not a strong enough word to use for how I felt about the changes that were happening to my body. They all started right before and continued after I got married. I could not find any doctors who could tell me what was going on. There were lots of theories but no solid diagnosis or help.

My sweet mother was so worried about me and had seen on television a doctor who specialized in hard-to-treat cases near where she lived. She knew where he ate lunch, and she waited in the parking lot to talk to him and begged him to help me. He agreed to see me, and finally, after so many years, I was diagnosed and treated by a metabolic doctor for a metabolic syndrome and mercury poisoning. The clinic was five hours from where my husband and I lived. For a year, we drove once a month to North Carolina and back home for me to receive special treatments from him.

During that time, I felt invisible again. I experienced what it's like to be overweight. You are seen but ignored, judged, and treated as if you are not intelligent or don't matter as much as someone thinner. Never being able to find clothes that fit right or you feel comfortable wearing. Feeling like your feelings are not as important. Being overweight by choice or not is treated by others like a disability. I am glad to see that today some of this is changing, and being heavier is not judged as harshly as it was twenty-five, thirty years ago. No matter what you look like, you still matter and are important.

For many years I worked on my health and weight but kept to myself a lot. All of my self-confidence was gone. I wanted to hide because things like seeing the disapproval of how I looked in my father's eyes was just too much. I already felt unloved and disapproved of by him, and it made me both sad and angry. Somewhere inside of me was this spark of light that whispered, I don't deserve to be unloved, I'm not that awful, am I? There was also the guilt of my poor husband watching me get bigger and bigger and more recluse, and there was nothing he could do to help me. Debilitating anxiety set in, and at times I could not leave my house. For a time, it was an endless cycle of misery—anxiety, eating, depression.

I am very grateful that with the help of the doctor in North Carolina, he was able to help me understand what was happening to my body so I could start to gain some control again. It took a while, but with eating only protein and vegetables, using chelation to get the toxins out of my body, and exercising after dinner, I was finally able to drop almost 100 pounds. My mental health was getting better, and my cycles started back. After seven years of marriage, I became pregnant. I had just started seeing an infertility doctor, and before he even tried any treatments, I was pregnant. This changed my life in more ways than I can say.

I now had a purpose for the first time in so long. I began to dream again of things I wanted to do in my life and with my life. After my first daughter was born and near a year old, I started a gourmet candy business. After my second child was born, I started a jewelry business that was very successful for five years. For ten years, I was on the PTO at my children's school. I did a lot of fundraising and marketing during those years. I learned so much, and the extravert that became a recluse came out once again. I started to discover myself once more. I threw myself into being a mother and being of service. I still use all that I learned from that time period in my life today. It was invaluable.

I continued to work on my mind and body, and at age 45, I found myself surprisingly pregnant. This birth would change my life again. The end of the pregnancy was very challenging, and we were not sure if our son would make it and if I would after the birth. In my recovery time, I went through many mindset shifts and analyzed my life and belief systems. In a state of complete gratitude one day came the words to my first children's book. Because of my inner dialogue of feeling invisible, I thought I would save what I wrote for my son someday. No one would want to read anything I wrote. I believed I was a nobody.

After two years of a nudging from my higher self and God, who has been with me through this whole journey, I decided to do something about it. I began to ask around about getting published. I was introduced to an author who wanted to write ten songs for my little manuscript. In 2017, we ended up getting published. We won a Gold Maxy Literary Award three months after the book came out, and the doors have continued to open.

I released my third children's book on June 2, 2021, and a midgrade reader September 2021. I co-founded and co-host two different shows on Amazon Live, and we are in our third year and not slowing down anytime soon. We've interviewed best-selling authors all over the globe, and our other show is all about the special needs and disability world. My autistic son and I do live educational videos with our public library, and we are starting a YouTube channel. I am also a ghostwriter and collaborator, as well as the voice on the Sports2Gether app.

Looking back, that invisible girl would never have imagined doing all that she has done. She could have stayed buried forever, but within each of us lies an internal power and strength. No one has the real power to take that away. And at the heart of every human is the desire to be heard and acknowledged. We buy into a false belief system when we are not sure of who we are on the inside. Through my growth, I learned that weight is a physical protection for our emotions, and it does not define who or what we are. I am now invincible forevermore. Sometimes it takes a while to find the brilliance which is within each of us.

Chris,

I hope you are inspired
by these stories

All the best,
Melodie Donovan
3/21/2022

CHAPTER EIGHTEEN

~

Believe In the Underdog
(it might just be you)

By Melodie Donovan
Coach, Melodie Donovan
https://MelodieInc.com

I believe in the underdog. I find myself drawn to the underdog. You know her. She's the one in the office that doesn't quite fit in. She's the one that has the strong opinion that most people don't like. She's the one that is not confident of her own abilities to succeed at her job. Sometimes she fails at a task she has been given. She is overlooked, misunderstood and not connected with the right people. She has worked hard for everything she has achieved. As hard as she tries, she still feels invisible. She sets goals for herself, but never takes time to revel in her victories.

There once was a young girl that grew up in a small rural midwest town. She was a girl of mediocre beauty. She worked hard in high school, mostly an A/B student, accepted in honor society, marched in band. She kept herself busy with activities. She had a dream! She wanted to be a high-powered executive or a New York fashion designer. In her little town it was very common for a girl to get married or be pregnant before her high school graduation day. If her dad had his way, she would be no different. She had her fair share of dates. But she had no intention of getting herself into either of those situations! She wanted more! So she worked and planned and worked and planned. Her dad only allowed her to apply to one state college. When she was accepted, he shrugged and dismissingly told her, "They are a state school. They HAVE TO accept you." This was her one chance to change the trajectory of her life from the normal and the expected. Even as she left home to go to college her dad said to her, "If you want to drop out of college to get married that's fine with me." In a moment of courage with determination in her voice her response was clear, "I will not be leaving college for any MAN!" She was determined to prove to her dad she had other plans. She wanted more than the norm of her small town's expectations.

College was harder than expected. The A/B student became a very average student. But she also had to work to pay for room and board and any other living expenses. Her parents paid for nothing!! She graduated! (hooray!) And while she was confident and proud of her achievements, she was not brave enough to head to New York a thousand miles away to break into the fashion industry. Instead, she headed to the big city in her home state, Indianapolis. It would be a safe start, one where she could encourage herself and motivate herself. If she failed; home wasn't too far away. But in her mind she knew.... FAILURE WAS NOT AN OPTION!!

She started in retail then moved to an office job. She started as a marketing assistant and moved up to assistant controller in 5 years. Unfortunately, the company was lost to mismanagement and bankruptcy. By this time she was married and had one baby to care for as well. Her dream of being a fashion designer was a distant memory. But she was the "ultimate woman" if she was measuring herself to the marketed expectations for women.... ENJOLI, You know, Enjoli perfume, "I'm a woman, Enjoli." (cue perfume jingle) "I can bring home the bacon....da da DA da... Fry it up in a pan....da da DA da and never let him forget he's a man.... Cause I'm a Wo---Man ENJOLI."

Wait!! There's more.... even on her wedding day as she looked at her soon to be spouse, she knew that this union would not be until death do us part. She had seen her future in a dream, a vision of her life, and knew this would not be for forever.

The vision showed her as a successful corporate executive with an office in a building in downtown Indianapolis. A single mom. A businesswoman.

But was she happy? Fast forward 20+ years. The work was long and tedious. She was working for a company where you had to know someone to get ahead. By this time she had been overlooked and passed over for three promotions. Each of the promotions went to a man with lesser qualifications. She was still fighting the same fight; women just didn't get the corner office. She was losing her confidence and they drove her to mediocrity by denying her an opportunity to advance her position. She sunk into invisibility. She thought, "Just keep your head down and don't ruffle any feathers. Get your time vested and then leave." Her invisibility allowed her time to plan and build her confidence. She started reaching out to find other women like her who were doing what she wanted to do. She wanted to be an independent entrepreneur.

Her children are grown. She taught them to go after their dreams. She supported and encouraged them, "You can do anything you want to do. It may not be easy. It may be a lot of hard work. I believe in you. Go after your dreams." And now as her boys are building their dreams, the encouragement has come full circle. They understand the loss of their parents' marriage was removing a road block for them to their dreams. Their mom broke a cycle of doing what was expected, what was the norm, to open a huge door of all the possibilities they could dream for themselves.

They ask their mom, "Why not chase a new dream?" If you are not happy with where you are, find out where you want to be and go to it. They use her own words against her, "You can do anything you want to do. It may not be easy. It may be a lot of hard work. I believe in you. Go after your dreams."

That mom... that businesswoman... that young girl from rural Indiana is me.

A lot of women I have had the privilege to meet this year are picking a word of significance as a theme for 2021. My word is COURAGE. Courage to keep moving in a forward direction. Courage to keep trying. Courage to take action... to break down barriers and change outdated expectations. Courage to make the leap of faith into entrepreneurship. I got stuck in the muck and I forgot who I was. I had to ask myself what do I want!? What do I like to do? Sometimes you get so far away from who you really are because you are trying to be what you think everyone else thinks you should be. You need to go back to your roots and the time in your life when you were happy. What were you doing? Where were you working? What did your workday encompass on a daily basis? What activities did you do for fun? Was it horseback riding, hiking, swimming? I found that of all the jobs I had the most fun and enjoyable days were those working for 2 entrepreneurs as their office administrator. I did a lot of research projects and worked independently a lot of the time. It was fun to talk through new business ideas and then research the viability of those ideas. A few we ran with and a few we held back to simmer a little more. Take time to think about these things. Journal your thoughts about them. Make a vision board. For years I thought vision boards were pointless. Boy was I wrong!! You have to get your dreams out in front of you and out of your head in order to make them a reality. I realize now that a vision board does just that. It's a springboard to provide a daily reminder of what your dreams are and where you want to go. It makes it a little more tangible. Mine is hung on the wall next to my bed. I see it when I go to bed each night and first thing when I awake.

Greg Reid once said, "A dream written down with a date becomes a goal. A goal broken down into steps becomes a plan. A plan backed by action makes your dreams come true."

Dream again.... Dream a bigger dream! Dream one size too BIG! Hope for something more. I realized I am an underdog. I accomplished a lot on my own. I didn't have connections to help me land the jobs I landed. I got them by showcasing my skills and experience. But over the years I've made connections. Those connections helped rebuild me when I was broken, when I was discouraged and when I didn't believe in myself. Yes, I was an underdog and maybe I still am. I also am someone who knows how it feels to be an underdog and I want to be what I needed when I was young. I can be a cheerleader and mentor for someone else. AND most importantly I encourage you to **Believe in the underdog because the underdog might just be you!**

CHAPTER NINETEEN

~

Hiding in Plain Sight

by Mischelle O'Neal
Founder/CEO, Mastering Your Monday LLC
www.masteringyourmonday.com

There is something so freeing about simply realizing the patterns that have kept you incapacitated and hidden for so long. That seemingly small realization allows you the freedom to feel a sense of hope and expectation for what the future could hold. The freedom to allow your mind to wander freely within the before illusive valley of hope. It does not negate the pains or the hurts suffered in the past, but it does open up a way for you to be free from their grasping hands in the future.

The sad thing is we often do not even realize we are being held in bondage until we are tightly entangled in the clutches of our warped reality. Realities of the lies I had built around me for so long that were based on a flawed, pieced together perception of a child's mind.

You are not wanted. You are not enough. You have to be perfect, good, and obedient to be lovable. You must prove yourself to have value. You must be perfect, unblemished, and have no flaws to be accepted.

No mistakes allowed on your watch, young lady! Not words that I can actually recall anyone ever saying, but they were the words playing out their siren song in my head. Words that drove my actions and my inactions. Somehow, if I could just do those things, be that person, I could be worthy enough to be accepted.

My story is not some horrifying trauma or catastrophic event. It is something that in many ways would be deemed insignificant. Funny how knowing a simple thing like, your father, the man who gave you seed, would not even acknowledge your existence, would not accept you, can have such a cancerous significance in your life. How it can tear away at the foundation of your confidence, value and worth. Small, insignificant phrases like, "God don't like ugly," and "good girls don't…" would literally make me want to shrink away, because I was not pretty enough, because I was not good enough. It was so hard to be a "good girl" to everyone.

And over the years these lies became harder and harder to fulfill. Those elusive demons forever driving my motivation, my thoughts, and my actions. I wanted so bad to be seen so I could be accepted, and if I was accepted, I had true value. I could be in a room of a thousand people, but if one face did not smile at me, did not acknowledge my existence, the 999 approving voices did not matter. I was rejected.

The two things that gave me solace in life were music and writing. Writing was how I could express the tortured thoughts that ran rampart in my head… and music, well, music is how I loved and how I sought acceptance. Everyone loves a performer, right? On stage I could be who they wanted me to be, give them what they wanted, be bigger than life and then I was free to walk away licking up the insincere gushing of their adoration, knowing that the person they were cheering was not me. Just a figment of their imagination.

Three hours after the emotional high, I was empty all over again. Like an addict. After a while, the pleasurable effects became harder to sustain. The ability to feed yourself the lie becomes harder and harder, and the high, well, that becomes shorter and shorter. I didn't feel safe playing full out, or rather, comfortable being me. So, I hid. That's right!

I hid in plain sight.

But one traumatic accident began the shift to turning things around. Funny how God works. Everything that day was carefully orchestrated, and I didn't even realize it. I had gone to work that day; my daughter was at school and I was on my way home to be there when she got out of school. I was alone driving down the highway after just getting my car registered for the upcoming year. Normally we're always together, but that day I was alone.

I was traveling about 50 miles an hour when an old Buick (I mean really old) pulls out from the shoulder right in front of me to make an illegal U-turn. I couldn't believe it! I didn't even have time to hit the brakes as I plowed into the side of their car head first. As I watched their car go airborne and begin to roll over in slow motion, it seemed in that same space of time my breath was pushed out of me as the steering wheel came barreling into my chest. That saying, "I saw my life flash before my eyes," well, it did! I am almost sure I heard the word "Jesus" escape my lips in a puff of air. And then, stillness.

I am not even sure what happened to me after that, at least not until I got to the hospital, but I do know it was at that moment as if someone had removed the scarred, scraped, cloudy lenses of the past from my eyes and corrected my vision. Oh, don't get me wrong. I kept trying to resort back to my old lenses, the ones I was comfortable with, even though in them, my vision was distorted. It was because I was familiar with the old lenses, and, well, the new vision, that clarity, scared the devil out of me (smile), maybe literally.

Funny how we stay in the pain of familiarity because of a fear and distrust of the unknown. How we are so willing to suffer a known pain, a known heartache, instead of grasping the lifeline that's right there in front of us. All we have to do is grab it and hold on. Every doubt of why what is right before our eyes will not work begins to play loudly in our mind. And even if we were able to grab the truth, if we do not hold on tight, it begins to slip away from our grasp.

The beautiful thing is, when you get just a glimpse of the truth, you begin to question everything that came before it. You begin to bring into question every lie you have been told, every story that you have told yourself in the past causes you to begin to question your whole belief system. What else could be a lie? And that begins a sometimes painful, but beautiful, journey to healing.

I began to reevaluate my relationships, those who I surrounded myself with. How they were feeding into me, what messages was I allowing to infiltrate my subconscious. Everything began to become under the subjection of my truth. I began to reshape my life. The stories were the same, but I began to reframe how I saw them. I learned to question my motivations and call out my self-imposed lies.

I wish I could tell you that there was some miraculous instant change, but I would be lying. It is a journey that even I am still traveling. I have been on this road for almost 30 years now and each day I have a new revelation, a new insight, a new shift. Just when you think you have come to the crux of your journey, there is another corner just ahead; another milestone to be conquered.

The beauty is, with each corner you turn you start looking expectantly for the next, and if you happen to look back, you begin to see just how far you've traveled. If there was any one word I would pull from my journey, I think it would be "*intentional.*" I've learned to think long and hard over the choices I make, the people I embrace in my life, and the actions I take. I've been able to let go of the things that held me hidden and I purposely choose the truth through exposure.

It is not easy. Each day is a struggle, one of battling the lies. But even they are getting fewer and farther between. I've learned to throw back the curtain, no costumes, no makeup, just a monologue from the heart, with heart. I'm no longer hidden; I've been exposed, and the beauty of being exposed is you no longer have anything to hide. So freeing! Why did I take so long?

I have burned those bridges! And I can't go back. I don't want to go back! Once you have been set free to the realities of the truth, it becomes the sweet music in your ears. A sweet melody that comes back over and over again to comfort and lift you higher. It becomes the new song you fill your repertoire of life with to fill you with joy!

Each morning I rise up with the victory of the previous day behind me and the promise of the new day before me because I am invisible no more, invincible forevermore!

CHAPTER TWENTY

You Changed Me

by Mistie Layne
Founder, Write 2 Ignite Women's
Empowerment Retreats
www.StepUpAndSpeakOut.com

What does it mean to be **INVISIBLE**? Technically, it means, *ignored, not able to be seen, not taken into consideration, and hidden.* Have you ever felt **INVISIBLE**? Have you ever tried to become **INVISIBLE** for one reason or another? My authority on this subject comes from a decade of beatings, hostage situations, and abuse—physically, emotionally, and mentally. I went from a confident Texas beauty queen studying to be a surgeon to hiding behind bushes, sunglasses, long sleeve shirts, lies and addiction. I lost my voice, my identity, my visibility and became lost, broken, and silent. However, the one positive thing I can say about that dark time of my life is that it changed me and made me strong, confident, forgiving and a fearless force to be the voice of those still in "hiding" and **INVISIBLE**. I am here to fight for you and teach you how to become strong enough to fight for yourself.

How does domestic abuse start? How do you know when you are in it? How do you leave? I wish I had known the answers back then, but after many years of therapy, soul-searching, forgiving and re-discovery, I am here to inspire and encourage you that you can overcome your worst to live your best. Do your research, gain education on the subject, and make a plan to better your life. I learned abusers will search for any tiny little insecurity we have and use it to dominate and control us. My abuser (my drug dealer I thought I was in love with) knew exactly how to manipulate me, he was a master manipulator. It started slowly and by the time I realized I was being controlled, I was in too deep (so I thought) and didn't know how to get away. I tried everything from kicking him out, to moving across the country to restraining orders, but he used scripture, our son and crack cocaine to keep me in his reigns. Believe me, as abusive and enraged as he would become, he was equally charming and convincing by saying he was sorry.

I started fading away into invisibility when I became addicted to crack cocaine after being left depressed and vulnerable from a divorce. I was a 32-year-old mother of two studying to be a surgeon and should have known better. I was drawn to the "escape" the high provided and when Joey came onto the scene, it got insane with paranoia, jealousy, and rages. The control started with little remarks of jealousy, then progressed to checking mileage on my car to checking my phone. When he called the hospital to check on me, he would call the landline instead of my cell phone and I later realized he was making sure I was actually at work. When I thought he was checking receipts to balance bank accounts, I realized he was tracking times and mileage. He became so controlling I couldn't even take my daughters in my car to Wal-Mart without his permission or "escort." He dictated my clothes, my food, my music, my everything. I became timid, meek, and unexpressive in fear of a beating. I wanted to curl up, hide and oftentimes wished I were **INVISIBLE**. I didn't want to be seen because I was ashamed I had allowed a man to hit me over and over again.

The beatings became public after the first year. He assumed people already knew and no longer avoided breaking my nose or punching me dead in the eye, regardless of me having to go to work at the hospital the next day. I got tired of pretending and making up stupid stories nobody believed. I was actually embarrassed and knew I was being judged for staying with him. My bestselling book, **What Goes Up**, has a chapter "Never say Never" about how we don't know how we will react until it happens to us. Never judge anyone because we just have no idea their circumstance. We need more compassion in the world, not judgment. The fear is real! I was scared to leave, I feared my life, I feared my family's lives, I feared sobriety, and I feared facing the woman in the mirror that I had become. Nobody recognized me anymore and I was scared of that girl in the mirror.

It wasn't until I ended up in prison for killing somebody behind my cocaine addiction that I realized how lost I was. Jail forced the physical separation that allowed me to start healing. I realized how much I had been biting my tongue in fear of the physical consequences when I said something he didn't like. I resented holding my tongue because I really wanted to tell him I hated every single fiber of his body and dreamt of breaking all 206 bones in his body. I visualized taking a sledgehammer and smashing him in the mouth so he could just once feel the pain he routinely inflicted upon me. I was no longer the strong, confident beauty queen wearing a tiara and sash waving in parades, instead I felt **INVISIBLE**, unimportant and that other Mistie was long gone with little hope of ever returning. He changed me and I resented him for stealing so many years of my life. However, I knew I had survived it all for a reason and decided to get busy and fight to live instead of fighting him.

I spent my time in prison writing my life story, which was the therapy that saved my life. I discovered my buried pain and took time to address, confront and conquer it all. I took accountability for the poor choices I had made in my life and then learned how to forgive myself and then others. Basically, I put the work in and soon realized I was a winner and now an authority on so many adversities I had overcome. The more focus I put on liking, then loving, myself, the stronger I grew. Prison put the physical separation between us, but I made the break from him emotionally all on my own. I realized I didn't love myself and didn't feel worthy of anyone else's love either. I started finding small things to love about myself and find gratitude in all the things around me, even from a tiny jail cell. I had made a mess of my life, but dammitt my life was far from over. I had to fight! You need to fight! Pull Yourself UP!!!

Once we discover our strengths from living through our adversity, we should STEP UP AND SPEAK OUT to help ease a little suffering in the world. Through sharing our experiences with transparency, we can JUDGE less and MENTOR more. By LIVING through it and now being on the other side of the adversity, I am **INVINCIBLE**. I AM A WARRIOR. Although biting my tongue was hard with the volatile storm of anger raging inside me, I am thankful I did because it kept me alive to be here today as a beacon of light in somebody else's storm. I can be the encouragement for others and show them how to STEP UP AND SPEAK OUT to use their voice and be triumphant over their adversity.

Yes, HE CHANGED ME! He created this powerful, experienced, driven woman full of love, passion and insight. He gave me the determination to FIGHT. Now, I want to fight for other women still stuck biting their tongue and tell them they no longer need to be **INVISIBLE**. There is hope. We CAN thrive without them and we CAN repair the damage and move forward. The emotional and physical scars may not ever go away, but they are badges of honor that we were NOT DEFEATED. We lived, we survived, and we evolved. We grew into our places and NOW we must grow into our destiny as well. Thank you abusive husband, YOU CHANGED ME—from **INVISIBLE TO INVINCIBLE!**

All of us have a story to tell, some deeper than others, but all equally important to the universe. My story has so many more layers dealing with the death of a grandbaby, abortions, perfectionism, rape, legal issue, destructive hurricanes, cancer and killing somebody behind a ten-year horrific cocaine addiction. I believe what sets a person apart is what they CHOOSE to do on the other side of their adversity. Are you sitting in the "victim" chair, the "pity" pit, or the guilt arena? If so, I challenge you to take that negative energy you are pouring into yourself and find somebody to direct it to and pull them up, just a little. The act of serving and focusing on others is the most rewarding I've encountered. If we all did our part by stopping the judgment, people-pleasing, lies, and façades and learned to be our authentic selves, the world would be so much better. Who can you help around you? What has made you a bad ass and **INVINCIBLE**? Have you even realized you have conquered an adversity and no longer need to dwell on it? Do you have a story to tell? If so, it's time to STEP UP AND SPEAK OUT with Mistie Layne.

CHAPTER TWENTY-ONE

~

A Fairy Tale – A Would-be Princess Finds Her Happily Ever After

by Nancy Lockhart
Founder, Lockhart Marketing
https://lockhart-marketing.com

In the late 80's, after graduating from college, I moved from Illinois to California with my then fiancé. He was training to be a sheriff in the Los Angeles sheriff's department. It was a huge gamble. I knew no one. I was just beginning my marketing career with no apparent leads. I was young and impressionable and I was in love. Unfortunately, I was also in an abusive relationship. My fiancé gave me black eyes, broken ribs, horrible bloody noses, and regular visits to the emergency room. At one point, after a particularly tough day at work, my fiancé held his gun to my head and dared me to call the police. Since he was a sheriff, both he and I knew that nothing would happen to him, and I would be considered a hysterical over-reactive girlfriend that was having a bad day. My fiancé would have answered the door and explained that we had had a misunderstanding. Flash that badge, they'd be on their way and I would be in for some fresh kicks, slaps and punches for embarrassing him. At that time, there were no laws that required law enforcement to investigate the complaint further. So, I just told him what he needed to hear and begged him not to pull the trigger.

Guess what? I married him even after all of that. I was a huge believer in the fairy tale. Prince Charming and happily ever after. Love conquers all, and as long as my Prince Charming knew that I loved him, we could get through anything. Even bad tempers, bruises and insecurity.

But, the fairy tale was not coming true for me and my Prince. I had started my career at a market research firm. I was an entry level analyst evaluating grocery store coupon programs. It was a job in my chosen profession. I was pretty proud of myself. With my new career, I gained confidence. I could support myself; I was enjoying what I was doing! I started to question my beliefs about marriage. What did til death do us part mean, especially when staying might mean my death might happen sooner than expected? I realized that being isolated from friends and family on the other side of the country was a perfect way for my husband to keep me under his control. Luckily my job and his job required that we work different shifts – he worked nights and I worked days. This gave me just enough opportunity to reach out for help. My company offered an Employee Assistance Program where I could contact a therapist anonymously and for free. The first outreach was scary. I had NEVER spoken the words – "I am being physically abused," but once I did, my ideas about my marriage started to change. After 3 ½ years, I decided, with a lot of help from my therapist, that it was time for me to move out of my California home and the façade that was my marriage and explore life on my own. I rented a small apartment and started my new life.

One day, at work, I was asked to meet with our CEO. He brought me downstairs and told me that they weren't making enough money to cover the budget and that he was going to have to let me go. I was defeated. I walked up the stairs to my office to collect my things and the receptionist said that I had a call. It's your ex-husband. I was determined not to tell him what happened. He would just tell me to come home. Quite the contrary. He called to tell me that his girlfriend was moving into our house. Then the Northridge earthquake hit a few weeks later. I lived in a town near the epicenter. Literally and figuratively, my world came crashing down. I was nobody's wife, nobody's employee. I couldn't define myself in the fairy tale. This wasn't how happily ever after worked. I was at a point where I had to make a decision. I could give up or get on. I chose the latter.

I found another, better job. I moved into a townhouse and got a cat. I worked my way up the corporate ladder. I started working on the strategy and development of the company's brands where I worked. I won awards for naming and was asked to present all over Southern California. I met and married my husband and we had two amazing daughters. We bought a beautiful home in Simi Valley California. I was doing exactly what I had always wanted. I was living the dream and I could finally see that my fairy tale was coming true!

My career continued to advance, but I began to feel unfulfilled at work. There was a gnawing feeling that things weren't fairy tale perfect. I knew that there was something more that I was supposed to be doing. I was really good at my job and was making considerable impact, creating brand and product positioning and successful marketing campaigns. But I was under-appreciated, undermined and unable to lead my team in the way that I wanted: in the way that would allow them to grow and advance in their careers. I left my corporate job to pursue a position at a brand strategy agency. I thought that this move would provide me with the ability to make a more meaningful difference. These people knew what I did. They knew how I made marketing relevant. I was desperately searching to fill the void I was experiencing.

Unfortunately, that job did not fill the void and I was let go after two years of trying really hard to make it work.

I fell into a deep depression, peppered with sleep walking and panic attacks. I wasn't going to therapy. I couldn't get out of bed. This wasn't supposed to be in my fairy tale life . I did everything I was "supposed to do." I was a good, smart person. I paid my dues. I had grown through the trauma of my first marriage. My family was confused and angry. I was letting them down and I was letting myself down.

Then, one day, I finally snapped. I thought to myself, "I've had enough of this! There has got to be another way!" Chasing after organizations wasn't providing me with connection to my purpose. It wasn't even giving me the clarity to find my own purpose or value. I was continuing to look externally for validation and I was letting myself get beat up once again, and this time, I had only myself to blame. So, I drew a line in the sand and started looking for a new path. I realized that I could only take myself so far, and I wasn't willing to continue living my life halfway. I discovered that my fairy tale needed a fairy godmother and that I was going to have to reach out and ask for help in order for that magic wand to work.

Even though it was really scary, I took my control back. I called my therapist and started regular sessions with her again. I built my first website. I took photography classes. I was reading and exploring my spirituality. I was re-reading books that I started when I was single. The words in those books now had new meaning. I was able to connect with them on a level that I had not before. I enrolled in a Law of Attraction life coach certification program, and I began to coach women. I could feel the enormous shift that my clients had after one coaching session with me. I was inspired. I realized that I had been doing this work with friends and family, but had never connected my coaching to a career. I was doing what I longed for, but couldn't define in my earlier years. I was helping clients who had experienced some of the same issues that I had experienced, looking externally for validation that could only come from within. Then I realized that many women struggle with these same issues when starting or restarting their own businesses or careers. I had the background to help women take back their power and rewrite their own fairy tale. I could leverage all of my corporate marketing knowledge with my coaching to help other women redefine themselves and their businesses, while finding their purpose and creating a direct path to greater success and profitability.

I learned that the fairy tale can come true, and while I still have days where my story involves unexpected challenges, I know that I am in charge of my happily ever after. I have always had the power, I just needed to rescue myself.

Here's to more life chapters with happy endings and continued growth!

CHAPTER TWENTY-TWO

~

Shrinking While Growing

by Paige Davidson
Owner, Fast-Track Health & Wellness
www.TheFastingPaige.com

As I was waiting in the drive-through of a popular fast food restaurant, a car full of adolescent boys drove slowly past me, hurling trash at my car and screaming obscenities and phrases that included 'fat pig' and 'yeah, eat more and get even fatter, you hog!" Humiliation and embarrassment kept me from picking up my lunch order; I couldn't face the look of pity on the poor restaurant employee's face as I sped past the window. I couldn't escape fast enough, trying to hide the tears that amplified my shame.

Abject cruelty. The only experience that is worse than the invisibility that morbidly obese women suffer in today's society.

After this cruel incident, I almost welcomed the familiar invisibility that I wore like a cloak on a daily basis. Morbid obesity in America is considered a character flaw. It feels humiliating to know that you are assumed to be stupid, at best, because how else could you allow yourself to become so fat? Pretending not to see the look of disgust on interviewers' faces, knowing that you will be passed over for yet another job that you are highly qualified for, is degrading and beyond disheartening. To know that the reason you are invisible to others is because they have no respect for you, they see you as less than, they assume that you are dirty and slovenly and even lazy, is to feel constant dejection and hopelessness.

I grew up in diet culture, both in my home and in society. I learned early on that in order to lose weight, you had to "go somewhere." Some diet doctor had to fix you, to tell you what to do, what to eat and not to eat. For over 40 years, I tried every weight loss center in existence. I began my weight loss attempts in high school, falling into a vicious cycle that would continue for many years with this same weekly weigh-in program. I joined, hopeful this would be the time that it would work. I tried my best for a while, suffering the embarrassment and growing sense of failure each week as I was weighed, forced to report my progress (or lack thereof) that week to the rest of the group, and eventually quit. Until the next time I was called fat, or ignored in a situation that particularly stung, or got so winded trying to climb a set of stairs that it frightened me. Then the cycle would begin again, the same process playing itself out as my self-esteem plummeted, until it was eventually non-existent.

Years' worth of various diets, exercise programs, doctor supervised liquid diets, physician prescribed weight loss pills, injections of who knows what, potions hyped to be 'the solution,' and diets that eliminated entire food groups later, weighing over three hundred pounds and physically and emotionally broken, I desperately submitted to the 'ultimate' weight loss scheme: gastric bypass surgery. I was the second roux-n-y gastric bypass surgery patient in Kentucky in 2000. I will never forget the surgeon saying to me, "Paige, I can operate on your stomach, but I can't operate on your brain." And that was it! There was no further information or assistance in this area.

Hearing this was terrifying, because I knew exactly what he meant, and I knew nothing at all about what he meant. Clearly there was something wrong with my thinking, but what? When you have thought the same way since you were a child, you believe that is just the way it is. What everyone thinks. What is normal. I absolutely could not identify how my thinking was flawed, or caused me to gain then lose then gain then lose, ad nauseam. The first step in healing is always awareness. How can you heal from disordered thinking when you have no idea how your thinking is disordered?

Providing me with the physical tool to assist me with weight loss, yet failing to provide me with the tools to change the lifestyle, mindset, attitude, and disordered thinking that led to morbid obesity in the first place bordered on medical malpractice! Yet who did I blame when the surgery was ultimately a failure? Myself, of course! Never mind the fact that if I had known how to 'cure' myself all on my own, I would never have been morbidly obese in the first place. My growing sense of failure continued to snowball.

Knowing that I was dying a slow death, one forkful at a time, I desperately set out to do something I had never done before; try to get healthy, not just lose weight. The very first thing I did was to declare that I was never going to diet again! Over 40 years of dieting had resulted in weighing 315 pounds at the time of my ill-fated weight loss surgery. I wasn't sure exactly how to proceed, but I did know for sure that a diet was not the answer.

I also decided to try another thing I had never tried before, counseling. I found a good fit with an amazing Christian counselor named Linda, and at our first meeting, I told her, "There is something really wrong with me. I either have a food addiction, or an eating disorder, or maybe I have OCD when it comes to food and eating. But regardless of what it is, I have to get it figured out, because I just can't continue to live my life this way."

Soon after Linda and I began our work, I learned of an amazingly healthy way of eating and managing food, called intermittent fasting (IF). IF is not a diet, although I did not believe that at first. In fact, I declared that it sounded like a crazy fad diet, and I wasn't doing it! However, I soon learned that besides not being a fad or a diet, it actually heals inflammation in your body. This got my attention, because I was suffering with acute pain due to plantar fasciitis in one foot, and Achilles Tendonitis in the other. I was in such severe, constant pain that I was limping. It was debilitating. Inflammation causes both conditions and this particular side effect of practicing an IF lifestyle captured my attention. After researching IF I discovered that it isn't indicated for those who have a history of eating disorders. I brought my research to Linda, and expressed my interest in trying IF. Not to lose weight, although by then I was back up to 250, precipitating my desire to begin counseling. Linda reminded me that we had no idea yet if I had an eating disorder and suggested that I try IF and if I found it helpful, continue it. If I didn't, just stop doing it.

With her blessing, I began right way. To practice an IF lifestyle is merely to eat your food in a period of time each day, called an eating window. Outside of your eating window you practice a clean fast. For example, one popular IF protocol is 18/6. Fast for 18 hours (including sleeping time!), and consume your food during your six-hour eating window. IF attends to when you eat your food, not what you eat. You focus on eating foods that you enjoy and that are good for you, and throw in an occasional treat, whatever that means to you.

Within six months, my painful foot conditions were 100% healed. And even more incredibly, I had also lost over 50 pounds! Finally believing that IF really wasn't a diet, I came to the shocking conclusion that I actually could lose weight without "going" somewhere, looking for someone to fix me.

Practicing an IF lifestyle was the beginning of an amazing new sense of empowerment, to take my health and wellness into my own hands. I kept going, and in 14 months had lost 110 pounds and many clothing sizes. Yet my weight loss was a footnote compared to the other benefits practicing IF brought me.

I learned to be an intuitive eater, learning to love healthy foods that made me feel amazing. I learned the importance of a positive attitude and mindset. I discovered that healthy habits are foundational to a healthy lifestyle, and I learned the critical lesson of what it means to truly love myself! Of critical importance was the fact that I actually learned how to stop the negative, mean self-talk and learned to show myself lots of grace, to be kind and loving and gentle with myself. This made all the difference in the world in the way I felt about myself and even my outlook on life! What I thought was yet another weight loss journey turned out to be a deeply spiritual journey with physical healing.

Ultimately, I learned that by becoming empowered to make good decisions for myself, I truly went from being invisible in the world, to being invincible – as a woman who is fully in charge of her own physical, mental, emotional and spiritual health!

CHAPTER TWENTY-THREE

~

COME OUT, COME OUT.... The Four Words That Took 20 Years to Say

by Pamela Gort
Founder, Lesbian Love Coaching
www.LesbianRelationshipCoach.com

Why had it taken me so long to tell my parents these 4 words—"I am a lesbian"?

Why were they so difficult for me? This defined who I love, it's part of me. It's who I am and yet I couldn't come out to them. It had been 20 years since I came out to myself, 20 years of leading a double life, my straight life and my real life. I was so afraid of being shunned, ostracized, thrown out of my family for fear of embarrassing them, ashaming them. Apparently, I wasn't afraid of shaming myself from being who I am. It took 20 years and a woman named Eleanor Palacios.

I had come out to myself and my gay world, but not to the people who mattered most or with whom I spent the most time. To my colleagues I made up boyfriends and told stories about dates I had been on that weekend. I didn't have a photo of my partner on my desk like everyone else. I told them as little as possible about my personal life so they would not get suspicious. I kept my world hidden from them for almost 20 years.

Many of us hold a secret or even a secret life. You do not have to be gay to be in the closet. Many of us protect ourselves with armor or keep silent about something that really matters to us. Perhaps one day some event or person in your life will inspire you to rip off the armor and reveal the secret that holds the key to the real you, the authentic person you were always meant to be.

I felt different, scared and alone for as long as I could remember. I was not sure why. I liked to play with "boy" toys and dressed in jeans and cowboy boots. My playground was outside, in the woods, and in the garage building things. I did play with Barbie dolls for a short time and secretly made the girl dolls kiss each other. I played sports and reveled in the competitive environment. I was a good Catholic girl, did well in school and didn't want to rock the boat. I played the game of being straight. I dated "boys" throughout high school and college. I fooled everyone around me and was miserable but safe from judgment and possible scorn. I tucked away girl crushes deep within hoping the feelings would simply go away. Occasionally I would fantasize about kissing one of them but never had the courage. In college when all my friends were in serious relationships, to fit in I even considered marriage.

Who inspired me to come out? Many years after college I was on an Olivia (lesbian exclusive) vacation in Mexico. Every morning I went for a run with a woman I had met named Eleanor Palacios. One day she asked me if I was out and I replied, "Yes, but not to my family." And she asked why. When I told her about my fear of being disowned, Eleanor said, "you're afraid that they will reject you, but can you see that you are doing the same thing to them, rejecting them? You don't even know how they will respond. And yet you choose to keep them from this most important, sacred part of you." Wow! That hit me like a two-by-four across the head.

I was already 10 years into a serious relationship, and we hid it without fail. When my parents would come to visit, we would "straighten up" so it looked like we each had our own bedroom. I would turn down holiday visits under the guise of wanting to go skiing with my precious vacation days. The truth was I wanted to be with my partner on holidays out and open to the world, so I lied. If I couldn't kiss and hug her in front of my family, then being there for the holidays wasn't an option.

No one ever accused me of being a bad person for being gay, but I felt ashamed or at least felt that they would be ashamed of me. The programming I had grown up with, especially from the church, told me that being gay was wrong and that there was something wrong with me. No wonder - The DSM (Diagnostic & Statistical Manual of Mental Disorders) listed homosexuality in its list of mental disorders until 1987. Was I so wrong for not coming out?

Those moments with Eleanor helped me realize that I was the one closing myself off. In that moment I decided to come out to my parents. It was time to come out of my closet, to reveal all of me. Coincidentally, my father was having hip replacement in October just a month away. I wanted to be there for my mother and so I planned the trip to fly across the country.

In the weeks that ensued I practiced what I would say. My inner critic and inner cheerleader laid out for and against arguments like a ping pong match in my head. I was so torn and almost gave up. What a terrible person I was to keep this from my family, to lie about dating men, to hurt my partner by introducing her as a friend. So much hurt and deception! How had this hurt me by hiding a big part of me inside for so long. As I vacillated, I knew that the fear I felt was fear of the unknown. I built up courage and dug deep to find compassion for myself every day.

Finally, the day came, October 11, oddly also National Coming Out Day (yes, there is such a thing!).

On October 11th, 1998, after flying from California to the East coast where my parents live, I came down for breakfast and told my mother I needed to talk to her. She was in a hurry to get to the hospital, but I persisted and eventually blurted out to my mother across the kitchen table - those four life changing words – and watched the tears fall from her eyes. What have I done, I thought? She did not reject, disown or ostracize me. Understandably, she worried that I might not have an easy life. She saw the prejudice, judgment and violence heaped upon the gay community. She showed her love for me even in her questioning acceptance. Referring to my sisters who had their husbands to take care of them, she wanted the best for me and she wasn't sure that being a lesbian was the best. I knew she needed time to think about this, to wrap her arms around it. One thing that I didn't doubt was that she would continue to wrap her arms around me and she did.

As we drove to the hospital, she made me promise not to tell my Dad until he got out of the hospital. That is the only reason I actually went, but it was convenient to kill two birds with one stone. And I was hoping I was not going to be one of the birds that morning. I had just enough time to be there all day to make sure everything was all right and to support my mom. But I needed to get back to work.

A week later, the phone rings and it's my father. I was afraid because I did not think my father would ever accept this. My father greeted with me, "Honey, I love you. You are amazing. There is nothing you could ever do that would take our love away from you." I almost froze as in that moment, all my fears, doubts, concerns, shame and guilt were wiped away and all was good. What my dad did for me was give me the courage to be me, all of me. From that moment on, I decided to come out whenever I could. I became the poster child for coming out. I would say, "hi, I'm a lesbian" like saying hello!

Years later at my dad's funeral, my sisters and I were sharing "Dad stories." I mentioned how cool he was to completely 100% accept me from the get-go. They looked at me in disbelief. Then they explained that at first he didn't. "He had such a hard time with it. He cried a lot." I was instantly shocked and mad that he lied to me, faking that acceptance. My sisters looked at me and said, "But don't you understand what he did. He took the time to understand it, to accept and love you. He wanted you to know that part."

Suddenly, I realized that my father had given me the best gift of all - the gift of unconditional love. We should have it for ourselves; I should have had it for myself then. The problem is society tells us how to be, how to act and how to behave and what is right, and what is wrong. I struggled with that because I wanted to belong. When we are different, we do not want to be rejected.

My father gave me so much that day that helped shape a more fearless life of being truly myself. I worked hard and was successful in corporate America as an out lesbian and then as a solopreneur and now The Lesbian Love Coach, a name I own with pride. Never again will I hide this part of me.

From this experience I saw the value of how adding compassion for myself could have made a huge difference and perhaps encouraged me to come out sooner. There are **3 sensory compassion tools** you can use when dealing with a difficult issue where you might be harshly judging yourself. First is an <u>auditory tactic</u> - to treat yourself like a best friend or child and say those warm soft things like you're okay, you're a good person, I love you, you did the best you could, it's okay. Use almost cooing sounds to provide a supportive feeling. Imagine what you would say to a friend who was berating herself and actually say those things aloud to yourself.

Secondly, take your own hand as a <u>touch tactic</u>, touch your forearm and even give yourself a big hug as if you were doing this to a best friend or child needing loving support. This physical touch helps to release "feel good" neurotransmitters which can soothe us and bring us into a calmer, more peaceful state.

Lastly, this one is a <u>taste tactic</u>. Fill a glass with water. Think of someone you love deeply and unconditionally. Imagine sending love to them via the water in the glass. Keep doing this infusing of the water with the love you have for the person for a few minutes. Now drink the "love infused" water and feel its power inside you. Feel yourself filling up with love. This tactic is called the Trojan Horse because it is a sneaky way of giving yourself unconditional love when you might not be able to just by thinking of yourself.

The lessons I learned from this experience was to have compassion for myself, and for others and what they are going through. Compassion for myself for not being able to tell the truth for 20 years. Next is to treat yourself like a best friend who really needs to get something out on the table. Tell them that it is okay. I needed to have compassion for my mother and father, who at first had a hard time with it, but came around. We can give people the time they need to accept things that are difficult for them because, ultimately, they will come around—some faster, some slower. Finally, the last and perhaps most important lesson is to be the true you, starting right now. If you have anything that you have been hiding, anything that you have been masking, if you are in a closet holding back your true self in any way, shape or form, come out, come out wherever you are. You will be better for it.

CHAPTER TWENTY-FOUR

~

The Power of Sharing Your Story

by Sally Green
Founder, The Self-Care Rockstar
www.TheSelfcareRockstar.com

Seventh grade sucks. That's all I have to say. I was devastated when one of the boys accused me of stuffing my bra. I tried to ignore him, but then he announced it to the class before the teacher came in. What didn't help my situation was that our classes were in clusters so I had the same kids all day long. I didn't cry. I just chalked it up to him being a stupid boy. I had four brothers at home, so I was used to being "teased," as they called it. Nowadays, it would be called bullying.

The next day I went to school thinking it would stop and that they would forget about it, but they didn't. It went on for months, every day someone would call me stuffy, or point and laugh at me in the hallway. I didn't tell anyone in my family. I was embarrassed and I felt that if I said something I would be harassed at home in addition to being tormented at school. No one at home knew what I was going through. I hid it very well.

Soon, even the girls in the class began to chime in. I began to withdraw. I would go home, sit in my room and read. Escaping into books became my therapy. I hated going to school. I hated those kids. I remember not being able to decipher whether events and daily occurrences were real or a dream. I thought about suicide. The thought of my classmates hearing about my death and being really upset for picking on me, somehow made me happy.

I had a Bible that I had received in third grade. Many days, I would come home after school and read stories from the Bible. I was hoping it would help me deal with the situation at school. One of my favorite books of the Bible to read was Proverbs. They were short little verses on how to live life. A lot of times I would just randomly open the Bible to a page and start reading. It always seemed that the page I landed on had something that helped me. Yet, the bullying continued.

Eighth grade was the same. Almost daily someone would call me "stuffy" or push me into the lockers while walking past me. I kept telling myself I was better than them, and that they would all grow up to be losers. One afternoon I was sitting in math class and one of the boys walked past my desk and whispered, "Hi Stuffy" and knocked my books on the floor. I finally broke down. I started sobbing uncontrollably and when the teacher walked in, I couldn't talk. He sent me to the guidance counselor.

I remember the counselor was a younger woman. She asked me what was happening and I told her what the kids were saying. She wanted to call my parents and have them come get me. I absolutely refused. I stayed in her office for the rest of the day and went home on the bus as usual. The next day no one said anything. One of the girls told me that the teacher had yelled at the class and that he was really upset with them. After that, things got better. But from then on and into high school I was quiet, withdrawn, and had a hard time making friends. I felt invisible.

When my daughter was about to enter middle school, I began worrying that something like that would happen to her. I wanted her to have a place to turn to if she or any of her friends were having any of the same issues I had experienced.

One afternoon, a customer told me about a group that was praying for a middle school Bible study. I got really excited because I thought this might be something that could really help middle school students, especially my daughter and her friends.

The next day the woman from the Bible study group called me. She said they were praying for people to join them and help create and design the Bible study. She asked if I wanted to be involved and I told her I would think about it. Although I had been a Sunday school teacher for close to 20 years, I had never actually attended a Bible study before. That night I couldn't sleep. I was thinking about all the Bible lessons I had taught over the years and how great it would be to teach them to older students.

The next morning I was driving to work and it was raining. I started praying out loud. (I had not prayed out loud in years.) I asked God if he wanted me to be involved and help with this Bible study. I told him I was really busy and had a lot of stuff going on. I didn't think that I could fit this into my schedule, but if it was something he really wanted me to do I would do it. As soon as I said "amen," there was a flash of lightning in a clap of thunder. I got goosebumps. Could that just have been a coincidence?

That night I decided to ask my husband what he thought. I was sure he was going to tell me not to get involved because I had too many other things going on. However, he was just as excited about it as I was, and told me it was a good idea and that I should do it. The next morning, I called Debbie from the prayer group and told her "I think I might be one of the people you have been praying for."

Debbie and I started the Bible study with six kids from our two churches. By the end of the first year, it had grown to over 20 middle school students attending our Bible study weekly. We called it B.O.B. which stood for "Break Open the Bible." By the end of our third year, the Bible study had over 50 students attending regularly and actually reading the Bible.

These kids were dealing with divorcing parents, being bullied, peer pressure, and thoughts of suicide. I remember one week a few of the kids came in and told us about a classmate who had committed suicide that week. We skipped our lesson and spent the class talking to them about it. Afterwards I looked at Debbie and said, "What the hell just happened?"

I grew so much spiritually during those years. I saw God talking to me in music and nature and coincidences or "Godwinks" (as I like to call them). After four years, that group of students moved onto high school and the Bible study abruptly ended. We tried to keep it going, but there was little interest. As Debbie and I talked about what to do next, I said, "Maybe we were placed here by God to help this particular group of students get through middle school, and now our job is done." I believe that is exactly what happened.

Creating that Bible study years after being bullied in middle school helped me to feel invincible. It would have been really easy for me to do nothing and not take action, but I am so glad that I did. It helped me grow in so many ways. And I can see now that by telling my story and sharing my experiences with those students, I was able to touch their lives.

I want to encourage you to share your story. You may think that no one wants to hear about what you've been through, or that your story isn't inspiring. But I can guarantee that there is someone, or a group of people, who desperately need your insight and encouragement right now. There are people who are going through what you went through. The only way to go from invisible to invincible is to lift others, listen to your heart, and take action.

CHAPTER TWENTY-FIVE

~

Not Invisible on Purpose

by Sarah Jung
Breakthrough Master Coach
www.SarahIsMyCoach.com

I was nine when my life changed forever, although I didn't understand it at the time. I was sound asleep at a sleepover at my aunt's when something woke me… something strange. It took a moment for my sleepy brain to register what was happening.

Someone was touching me.

I was too scared to open my eyes, too scared to even think what this might mean.

I knew there were only two men it could have been: my uncle or my cousin. To this day, I have no idea who it was.

And it was this event that silenced me for the next 28 years.

When I was eleven, my mother died in a car accident. My father, who is the most amazing, supportive, loving dad, told me, "There's no need to be sad because your mom went to Heaven. We'll see her again."

And I took that in. I made the decision that I would not allow myself to feel any feelings, so I squished them down deep.

Silenced. Again.

I had a cousin who was married to a pastor. He would occasionally drop by my house and ask me to make Korean instant noodles for him. He was always saying that I was so pretty and that he liked the way I made the noodles. I had learned to cook after my mother died, and I would do that for him because he was family.

When I was twelve, I was sleeping at their home. That night, I heard the door open to my room. This pastor laid down next to me and started to kiss me.

I thought, "I need to do something so that this doesn't go any further." So I moved, to let him know I wasn't asleep.

He said, "What's wrong?"

The only thing I could think to say was, "I have a headache."

"Oh, do you need some medicine?"

"No, I think I'll be okay."

And he left the room.

In the morning, when the family went out to get groceries, I immediately called my dad. Without asking why, he just came and took me home. I told him what happened, and the first thing he said was, "It's not your fault. And I'm not sure how, or when, but I will take revenge."

The most wonderful thing my father did was, if there were any family functions, he always asked me, "Do you want to go? He will be there. You don't have to go." He allowed me to choose to stay away if the pastor was there.

Because my dad believed me and supported me, I never felt the need to tell anyone else. My father's trust was sufficient to ease my fear and made me feel safe.

About four years after the incident, it dawned on me that I had stopped cooking. I also cut my hair and became a tomboy in an effort to not be pretty, although I didn't understand why at the time. I would get angry at any boy who said I was pretty. My immediate thought was always, "If you think I'm pretty, what are you going to do to me?" The more I felt that boys were attracted to me, the more I pushed away. I wore baggy pants and sweatshirts and did everything I could to make myself less pretty.

When I was sixteen, I was training alone in the gym where I was learning Tae Kwon Do. Some guys started catcalling through the glass doors. It sparked the rage in me, and I chased them, ready to beat them up (because I could).

Luckily, one of my instructors caught me first. He told those guys off, and then returned to me. Now, he was a big man, and I am a small woman. He picked me up and shook me and said, "What is wrong with you?"

And I had an epiphany. I "connected" what had happened to me with my rage. I cried. He cried. His compassion allowed me the space for the first healing breakthrough I ever experienced. I decided that I was not going to allow that one incident to affect me like this any longer.

I made a choice to forgive and forget, but that was not easy. I struggled for years. Fast forward thirty years. Although I had two kids with a disinterested husband and a personal life in the toilet, I had fully developed my business as an Education Consultant and Academic Coach for students on an accelerated journey to get to college.

In 2016, a member in a business coaching group on Facebook posted that he was offering a 30-minute discovery call. I scheduled it simply out of curiosity.

In that call, we did a visualization exercise. After about 15 minutes, he said, "It sounds to me like you're stuck."

"Yes," I said, "that's exactly how I feel."

He had me visualize myself in a forest and had me keep going. What do you see at the end?"

"It's dark," I said.

"And what do you think will happen if you keep going?" he asked.

"I'll die," I said simply.

Then he had me pave a different road. This time I felt I was on a stage, under a spotlight, and I could hear people clapping and shouting.

"How do you feel here?" he asked.

"Much better than the other one!" I said.

"You probably know what will happen if you keep going the way you have been," he said. "Your face just lit up on the second path."

And that's when I intuitively knew that I had to make a final decision on my marriage. I was exhausted from no communication and no support. I threw in the towel. I told my husband I was done.

The divorce happened, and I decided to work with my fellow group member as my coach. He took me through the NLP process to understand how everything from my past had affected me. People would see me and say, "You look so much happier and less stressed. What's going on with you?" I couldn't really explain my breakthrough because NLP was so new to me.

In 2019, I entered Practitioner Training, followed by Master Practitioner Training, and now I'm a Certified Master Practitioner of NLP, Timeline Therapy, and Hypnotherapy. During the training, I of course realized how his techniques had worked for me. Now I utilize those techniques with my students and clients.

The best part is that I get to see healing in others, just like I experienced. I went through tons of inner healing, and even had physical manifestations of stress clear up, like acne and irregular periods. Best of all, my ability to communicate has improved dramatically, and I no longer fear making my feelings known (which is something I did not do in nine years of marriage. No wonder I was stuck.).

I decided to expand beyond academic and college consulting and offer the life-changing Breakthrough Coaching to students and parents, many of whom are successful professionals. Many of them still suffer from guilt, trauma, and inner conflict that leads to outer conflict with their families, specifically their children. In my work with students, I have witnessed that many of their problems stem from the parents.

I'm a parent myself, and this whole breakthrough experience improved my relationship with my daughter who is 9 and my son who is 12, more than I can put into words. Once I resolved my issues, I stopped having issues with my kids. Before that, everything irritated me. I was always thinking, "What is wrong with them?" Now I can just love them.

That's why I developed the *Fast Breakthrough Experience*. This is a two-day retreat. In a nutshell, clients check in and 1. Get to take a break from their daily lives, 2. Get to focus just on themselves without distractions, and 3. Participate in the Breakthrough Process in which I ask targeted questions to bring out each issue and clear it. Some people already know what their issue is, like anger, guilt, or shame. But others, like myself, don't really know what's going on – only that there is a problem. And there just isn't enough time in the day to deal with it all.

Therein lies the beauty of NLP. You can literally clear years of fears, old patterns, and programming, limiting beliefs, and negative emotions within hours. It sounds magical, I know, but it actually has sound neuroscience behind the techniques. I'm living proof.

I encourage mothers to stand up and empower themselves first. This will empower your children to do the same. No more living in the shadows of other people. No more cowering on the sidelines. Step up. Speak up. Be visible. Find your purpose. Enjoy your life. Love your children. You deserve to feel the joy.

CHAPTER TWENTY-SIX

⌇

It's Time to Stand UP and Stand OUT!

by Sherri Leopold
Founder/CEO, Dream BIG with Sherri Leopold
www.ThriveWithSherri.com

We are made for a life of joy and fulfillment, but we need to have a strong voice, a sense of self, and genuine self-love to be fully happy. These three principles will determine your level of success and guide you towards invincibility! I will describe my journey using these three principles to live a happier, more successful life of influence and impact.

As a child who grew up in divorce, blended families, and chaos in the form of domestic abuse, it took me until I was twelve years old to find my voice. I had a voice; I simply didn't understand I could use it. Today I help people Stand UP and Stand OUT in their lives and businesses. I help them find that voice they have silenced, that caused invisibility. I see people like I see art. There is beauty in everyone, we just aren't everyone's choice. The most important thing we can do, though, is to be OUR first choice. Choose YOURSELF over anyone. If not, you'll likely become a tumbleweed.

The tumbleweed philosophy is how some have created their lives. If you think of a tumbleweed's behavior, blowing along, running into things, reacting. If it gets stuck, it's unable to dislodge itself. If it is in the wide-open spaces, it blows whatever direction the wind forces it to. This is a life lived without purpose or plan. One goes through life, running into jobs, people, situations, reacting and reacting again, over and over. A tumbleweed is a dead bush that meanders through life in reaction mode. Invisible people live this way daily.

INVINCIBILITY PRINCIPLE #1

Find Your Own Voice
It is always the loudest voice you will ever hear. Speak well. Moving away from the home where I witnessed the domestic violence at 12 years old was how I found my voice. In that home, I wanted to be invisible. Leaving there, I realized there was a different way to live. I could choose a calm, loving environment. I told my dad that I was tired of living in the chaos, which is what facilitated my move. I realized I had a voice. I always had one, I just didn't know how to use it. I spoke up, and it caused my circumstances to change. I stopped being the tumbleweed that simply reacted with fear, avoidance, and shame. I became a very social person once I was freed from my unstable environment. I was no longer afraid to be SEEN or HEARD! I realized I had value and what I had to say had value. You deserve to be heard. It's not whether "other" people think what you say is important, it's that YOU feel it's important to speak and what you say does matter. Speak UP, YOU are extraordinary. Do it for yourself!

INVINCIBILITY PRINCIPLE #2

Find Your Sense of Self

You can find it at any age. If you don't have a sense of self today, you can find it tomorrow. After 20+ years in network marketing leading many large teams, I have met all kinds of people. I really love people, all kinds of people. When Facebook became so popular, I joined. It is a social network, and I loved being social. I not only connected with people I knew, I began to connect with incredible people all over the world. These people did all kinds of fabulous activities, from writing blogs, starring in TV and films, and writing books. Many were coaches for personal development, finance, and business.

In 2018, I created my Dream BIG with Sherri Leopold platform. I began speaking on and leading the Stop Self-Bullying Movement. Throughout my life, I realized one of the greatest obstacles to someone's success is their inability to overcome their negative self-talk. I will cover this self-bullying next in the third principle. The most successful people loved themselves exactly as they were. These people stood out amongst the masses in my growing network. During a conversation with a friend, I asked if they knew a certain person. They did not. I felt like everyone should know these amazing people!

Pondering what I could do about that, I decided I could interview them! Facebook Live had become popular, so I decided to use that platform. I wanted to shine a light on these incredible people who were making a difference in the world, servant leaders. These people work every day to make an impact–definitely invincible. They choose impact over income. I created Outside the Box with Sherri Leopold which aired as a Facebook Live show. I enjoyed sharing these people with my personal network. Opportunity presented itself to share in a larger way, so I said yes without any hesitation! I wanted to stay with the same mission of revealing incredible human beings to the world. I am blessed to do this on a global stage now! I will honor this gift by developing this platform for others to shine and create the space for others to Dream BIG! Each episode contains someone who is creating space for someone to grow, change and improve their life in some way. It might be by creating opportunities for someone to write a book, become a coach, share a product, or perhaps even invent a world changing product.

One might wonder why I choose to shine a light on others, when I am talking about creating a sense of self. For me, I am filled with joy when I can see and help someone shine and show off their gifts and talents. I love to see them loving themselves and standing UP and standing OUT! This is truly what causes me joy. I love being part of their journey to success. The Outside the Box with Sherri Leopold show is true joy. I get to highlight those who are living out their passion. These people are purposefully denying a tumbleweed lifestyle! When you know who you are and stand in your purpose, people are never confused about who you are. I am a person who loves helping other people stand out. This IS who I am. It IS my sense of self. I am a champion of other people!

INVINCIBILITY PRINCIPLE #3

Have Complete Self-Love

I touched on it when I talked about the Stop Self-Bullying Movement. This movement was created specifically to teach people to love themselves exactly as they are with no qualifiers. Someone doesn't need to lose 20 pounds, get the best job, or find the perfect mate before they are okay or successful. When we can create an existence where we are happy with ourselves, there is then room for someone else. I frequently say, "others cannot out love us." A significant other, family member, or any other person can only love us to the degree we love ourselves. If we stand in the space where we are body shaming and degrading ourselves, we will attract others who do the same. Those who try to love you more than you love yourself, will become fatigued at constantly working to convince you of your worth. When you are aware of your greatness, you will attract great people. Perhaps you are even MORE awesome than you realize!

We will attract more of what we focus on. This is the reason we must KNOW our strengths, why we are unique, and our special talents. In our weakest moments, we must OWN and stand in our greatest strengths! It will keep us out of Tumbleweed-ville.

An important part of knowing and understanding yourself, speaking up for yourself, and loving yourself fully is understanding completely how unique you are. Your unique DNA is found nowhere else on this planet. If you ever feel you aren't unique, or that there is nothing special about you, you couldn't be more wrong. In fact, you are SO unique that no matter what message you feel you deliver, or what talents you have, no one else will or can ever deliver it like you! No one can compare to you! It is an irrefutable fact that you are an unrepeatable miracle exactly as you are! This is the type of person I have surrounded myself with for years, and the type of people that I want to share with others.

I will never again feel small or invisible. It is my choice to be invincible!

I invite you to follow along, Dream BIG, impact the world, and live your life on purpose and love yourself Big along the way! It's your time to Stand UP and Stand OUT! Find your voice and…

NEVER forget…

YOU are an unrepeatable MIRACLE!

CHAPTER TWENTY-SEVEN

~

The Ups and Downs of an Interesting Life

by Suz deMello
Bestselling, Award-Winning Novelist
http://www.suzdemello.com

Awhile back, I went to the Women's Fiction Festival in Italy. I found myself at dinner with writing coach Beth Barany and a couple of other friends. After a few glasses of wine and an excellent meal, Beth asked us, "What kind of life do you want?"

One writer stated, "A creative life," not unexpected in a group of authors. My friend Laura answered, "An independent life." I said without hesitation, "An interesting life."

By this point we all knew everyone else's personal history, and the statement was met by laughter—folks knew my life had been very interesting. Though I hadn't thought about it then, I've thought a lot about it since.

I have indeed lived an interesting life, holding several different jobs and embarking on careers ranging from trial attorney to romance author to yoga instructor. Perhaps my most interesting year was spent in China, teaching English to toddlers. But all of these were really nothing more than flailing about, the wanderings of a person who didn't know herself.

There's a reason for that. My parents' generation viewed children, not as independent beings, but lumps of clay to mold. A big part of myself is a persona I call "The Dutiful Daughter." I spent decades trying to please my mom and dad, especially my demanding father. A big fan of the old courtroom TV show *Perry Mason,* he believed that his studious, verbal daughter could have a bright future as an attorney. So I attended law school. Despite a D on my Civil Procedure midterm, I became editor of a law journal and clerked for a judge.

But I wasn't a particularly good student. I helped others excel by partying a lot, even on weeknights. At the height of the disco-and-coke craze, I'd go out to dance, closing down clubs before falling into bed at three a.m.

Untreated, undiagnosed depression will drive a person to behave excessively, seeking to feel good, better, even just normal, even though the behaviors are anything but.

After law school, I still struggled. Though I was offered a job or two, ethics prevented me from taking offers I couldn't stomach. So I opened a solo practice. Few succeed at this venture. Many lawyers who practice alone abuse drugs and alcohol, and I was not an exception. Though I was in psychotherapy, I was still lost within myself and utterly miserable.

Practicing as a trial attorney is like being a soldier—there are long periods of boredom punctuated by events of unbelievable stress. But I was good. I won more jury trials than the average. But I wasn't a good businesswoman and teetered on the edge of financial ruin for years.

I got lucky. After I married, my dentist husband and I discovered we didn't need my income. I had started writing, and after I sold a couple of books, I closed my law practice with a sigh of relief I felt down to my toes.

This event would have marked my "happily ever after" had I lived... happily ever after. But a few years later, a series of disasters struck at the same time.

My golden retriever died from cancer. Those readers who don't own a pet (or are owned by one) won't understand how devastated I was, but anyone who treats their dog or cat like family will. I had raised Blondie from a puppy and was closer to her than I was to any human, even my husband. I loved her so much that I would fondly regard the parts of my house she'd chewed—she'd eaten banisters, carpet, siding—whatever she could when she was a frustrated puppy.

Writers will understand my pain due to severe writers' block, from which I have never recovered.

Anyone will understand that I was shattered when I learned that one of my dearest friends, a woman whom I'd regarded as an older sister, committed suicide along with her husband.

And anyone will understand how I felt during the year after my eldest brother had been diagnosed with metastatic renal cell carcinoma.

After Keith's diagnosis, I bounced between my home in Sacramento and his in San Diego, trying frantically to spend quality time with my brother while keeping the threads of my life from unraveling—without success. I was also undergoing menopause, a massive chemical shift in a woman's body. There was an upside—eventually, when my hormones calmed, I realized that the cold, gray blanket of my depression had gone forever.

But while everything was happening all at once, I was a wreck. Not visibly—my family is British, and we Brits stiffen our upper lips and carry on. But I was falling apart, and because I was falling apart, my husband, who I now believe was co-dependent, fell apart also, and therefore our marriage fell apart.

2006 was surely my *annus horribilis*. After Keith died in May, I didn't have to shuttle to San Diego anymore, but my husband had decided our marriage was over. I wanted to deal with our issues and still feel that we could have stayed together happily. But though our marriage was my first, it was his third, and looking back, I now believe he'd planned for our divorce.

When the going gets tough, the tough get going, so I went—halfway around the world. I loved to travel. My love of travel had been born when I was little. Our parents took us overseas to meet our British family and see the sights—everything from DaVinci's *Last Supper* to Napoleon's Tomb. I rode a camel in Israel and climbed up to the Acropolis and Parthenon—tourists were still allowed to wander the ruins back then.

I spent a couple of months in Europe, where I truly feel at home, but it's a pricy place and I had no income. So I flew to Thailand, and in that inexpensive, friendly nation—don't they call it the Land of Smiles?—I started to recover. Slowly, in a 15x15 foot cold-water apartment, I began to heal. I wandered the streets of Chiang Mai, a city of heat and dust, dreamy temples and ancient city walls. I started to write again and produced the bulk of my two dozen books.

But nothing lasts forever. After six months away, my cash ran out, so I had to leave (reluctantly) for the USA. I had to finish my divorce and figure out what to do with my life.

Back in Sacramento, no one would hire me as an attorney. And why should they? I hadn't practiced law for nearly a decade. The financial downturn was beginning. Jobs were scarce. I got divorced, bought a home with the proceeds, worked at Starbucks as a barista and in downtown Sacramento as a grantwriter. But even with two jobs and owning my condo outright, I still couldn't make ends meet. And I was exhausted. I'd come in from one job, fall onto my bed for a brief nap, change my clothes, and go to the other job.

I couldn't go on like that, so I pursued a long-standing dream. I took my last five grand and returned to Thailand, where I earned a credential in teaching English as a second language. I spent that year in China, then returned to the States confident and renewed. After a lengthy stint caring for my elderly mother, who is afflicted with Alzheimer's, I found myself.

When Mom's illness got to a point where she was beyond my meager talents as a caregiver, my surviving brother took over. Luckily, he'd trained as a rehab counselor and even interned in an Alzheimer's care facility. When he divorced, he decided to change his life completely and moved with Mom to the beach in Mazatlán, Mexico. I followed, moving to Mazatlán about a year after my brother and my mom. They are the last remaining members of my nuclear family and are precious to me.

Now: I still am severely blocked but reconciled to that state. I have enough money to get by, being a person of modest tastes. But a modest income in Mexico will still get a person a lovely condo on the beach. I'm in the same building as my family, and I see them every day. I walk on the beach, cuddle my dogs, and write romance. Perhaps it's not the most interesting life, but I'm calm, stable, and happy.

While I've had an interesting life, and many setbacks, I can't complain about how everything has turned out. The great wonderment of my life is that I have made so many mistakes, so many wrong turnings, but still—everything is perfect. I'm the happiest, luckiest person I ever met.

At that same conference in Italy, I chatted with Karin Stoecker, a long-time editor at Harlequin UK. I told her my story and she exclaimed, "But you triumphed!" After a startled moment, I said thoughtfully, "Yeah, I guess I did."

Not all that glitters is gold,
Not all who wander are lost.
— JRR Tolkien

CHAPTER TWENTY-EIGHT

~

The Internal Conflict Called Introversion

by Trayce Young
Victory Coach, Trayce Young

Have you ever been in search of something and it seemed as if you just couldn't find it anywhere? You searched high, you searched low; all to no avail. Then, once you stopped searching, you found it. Have you experienced that? I surely have, time and time again. As I think on this, my mind moves from the tangible things I've searched for, like my keys or my cellular phone to some intangible things like self-worth and acceptance.

As I take a mental flight and reflect on all I have been in search of, one thing that comes to mind is visibility. From the time I graduated high school to starting my career in 2000, I remember bouncing from this job to that job; from this college to that college...all in search of visibility.

Thinking back reminds me that I was trying to fix the image of me. I wanted to appear as ready and confident. I wanted to show up as strong and sure of myself. However, deep down inside, I felt as if I didn't belong. To be honest, I have always felt as if I don't fit in. I didn't fit in at home. I didn't fit in at school. I did not fit in during my college years and I didn't fit in on my jobs. Why not…because I was not being authentic. I was presenting myself as how I thought I needed to, so that I would be liked and appreciated.

When I ended up working in the education system, I thought I had found what I needed to be doing in life. I imagined my family would be pleased with my decision of taking the job of a high school secretary. (I thought this because my mother is a retired teacher.) I wanted dearly to meet her approval. I wanted to show her that she could finally be proud of me. You see, since I didn't feel as if I fit in at home, I never felt that I could measure up. This feeling wasn't put on me by my parents. They were always so supportive of us girls.

I was born into a family of three daughters. I am the middle child. My feelings of not fitting in were brought on by myself. In my mind, my oldest sister had a place to land because she was the oldest. I knew my younger sister had a soft spot to land because she was the baby. However, I did not know and understand where exactly I was to fit in. If taking that job made my mother and father proud, it would be all I needed. So I thought. Wait though…was "I" proud of me?

Although I was in the educational setting, fulfillment did not come with that new secretary position. While visible to the students and staff at my assigned schools, I was still invisible to my true identity. There was still a void that had not been filled. I was experiencing an identity crisis. So, my search continued.

As I searched, I felt like I was in a cave. Somewhere dark, cold and unfamiliar. My cave was as a rocky womb. My cave-like experience was uncomfortable and calming at the same time. You may wonder how it could be both. Well, it was uncomfortable because I was alone. It was also calming because I was alone. You see, I have always desired to fit in. However, the introvert in me has fought that desire. The "introvert" Trayce wanted only to be to myself. The "introvert" Trayce wanted me to present myself as this independent, strong lady who didn't need anyone. That presentation kept me alone and comfortable. Wow, what conflict.

My cave-like experience left me feeling helpless, hopeless and untrusting. I no longer trusted myself because I could not rely on me to stop showing a fake ID. In that state of being, it was as if I would yell and yell, hoping that someone would hear my cries for help. I would even wave my arm rapidly to garner more attention. Mentally I was saying "Hey...over here!" Crickets. I thought, let me try again. Hello?...hello?...hello!!....NOTHING. No responses. There was complete silence other than my own voice being echoed back to me. No movement other than the shadows of my own arms falling back down to my sides. Imagine that for a moment. Imagine feeling alone and unheard; yet, feeling hoarse and tired from all the yelling. Surely someone heard me? How could they not? I felt myself becoming angry. How dare "they" not hear me. How dare "they" not see me. How dare "they" not acknowledge me?

They? Who is "they?" They are all of the family, friends and acquaintances I allowed to paint or create a narrative for me. "They" are all the people who have not asked me to rise higher in my true calling. What I soon realized is that I did not need others to hear my yells and rescue me. I needed to hear my own self and set a standard for ME to reach. When I chose to admit that I knew I was called to higher, I began making the necessary changes. I made a promise to myself that I can and will bet on me. I owned the fact that I had to do the work. NOTHING in life is just handed to you. The bible tells us that faith without works is dead. So, I vowed to myself that I would show up for me and dream again.

I am writing to tell you about my purpose. I am writing to share with you MY story. See, prior to 2018, I was comfortable with where I was in life. I was merely existing instead of living and thriving. As I took an account of my life, I realized that my true fulfilment and all that I had been searching for was right before my eyes. I have always dreamt of being Dr. Trayce Young. To see that dream come to fruition, I had to go back to school. Yes, this lady who was used to enrolling in several colleges but quitting them all would have to trust herself enough to see it through this time. I told myself, "Trayce, you cannot quit anymore. This is it."

Malcolm X reminded us that education is the passport to the future. In order to be educated I first had to loosen and dismantle the brick of indoctrination that enslaved me. I had to build my mind brick by brick by brick to trust and believe that I had it in me to pursue and accomplish. I had to take time and do the work of mindset shift.

I enrolled in college for the first time in decades. It was my fifth college to date. Ashamed, maybe. Transparent, yes. At the time of enrollment, I had enough credits to be classified as a junior. I decided to take the Fast Trac route because I knew that time was not on my side. I put my head in those books and I did the work. As I continued, I celebrated every single win. I had to. I needed to. In doing so, I was gaining confidence in me. I was learning to trust me.

I completed my bachelor's degree in 2019. I could hardly believe it. As I did, I realized that I now saw me as my authentic self. I also realized that I was no longer invisible to others. They could see my true identity as well. After taking that all in, I decided to bet on myself again to purse a Master's degree. Oh, trust and believe that self-doubt, fear and anxiety crept in. I had to ask myself, 'are you going to stop and put your dream back on the shelf or are you going to keep going?' I chose to keep going. I continued to work hard and earned my master's degree in 2020. I spoke affirmations to myself to keep the motivation going. I

KNEW I was being called to higher. I KNEW I had to continue toward my dream. There could not be any more time wasted on settling. Once I earned that degree, I thought…nothing to do but to keep pursuing. In February of 2021, I enrolled in a doctoral program. I knew that if I stopped long enough to ponder and question my grit, that I would most likely talk myself out of continuing. A question I asked myself earlier…am "I" proud of me? Now, most definitely!

If I can do it, anyone can! We just have to push past the doubt, negative thoughts and fear. We have to know our worth and understand the value of the gifts we carry. Invincible is defined as being too powerful to be defeated. You know what? I am TOO powerful to be defeated. I now boldly walk in that power with assurance. I am invisible no more, invincible forever more.

CHAPTER TWENTY-NINE

Authentically Me

by Whitnie Wiley
Founder/CEO, Shifting Into Action
www.ShiftingIntoAction.now.site

I f you would have asked anyone who worked with or observed me if I was invisible, they would have said, no. How could you possibly be invisible when you are on this grand stage doing amazing and important work? That understanding of visibility goes directly to the point of why I felt invisible. What I was doing was not about me, it was about the work. While I was in it, that was okay. Once I stepped away, I could see it didn't serve me.

That visibility, that voice was not mine. Mine was subjugated in deference to the work. The interesting thing was that until I separated from that situation, until I was out on my own, I didn't even realize that I had been silenced. But in reality, I had been silenced, operating under the radar for much longer than my time in that job.

The time I started consciously dimming my light coincided with my academic dismissal from the University of California at Berkeley. I had transferred to Berkeley after two years at community college on my second stint as a college student at the ripe old age of 18. I was 16 when I graduated from high school a year early, against the advice and counsel of my father who thought I wasn't ready. The rebel inside wasn't going to hear that. The fall after high school I started college at San Francisco State.

I only stayed one semester before transferring to Long Beach State to be near a guy I'd fallen for over the summer. The relationship didn't last long, and I returned home after a year of bumming around to start over at a community college. After two years, I transferred to the University of California at Berkeley, what my father told me to do in the first place.

It was a struggle from the start. Not sure if it was because it wasn't what I wanted or it was just hard. In any event, after the first year I was on academic probation and after year two I was dismissed. Crushed, embarrassed and lacking any self-confidence, I hid my shame about my academic status and just sort of continued with my life as if all were well. Not long after, I fell in love with someone else and got married.

A few years later, after my marriage fell apart, I again found myself keeping to myself because the advice I'd received prior to getting married was—don't. I stuffed my emotions and endured the pain in silence.

Hiding had become a habit. It's easy to walk through life with a mask on, pretending it is all working. But in reality, it's hard work. Over time it wears you down. If you are lucky, you walk away with only a few years feeling unseen and unheard, but the consequences for many are much worse. Your mental health is at risk when you are not living your life authentically. The life you were created to live.

However, I didn't voice my feelings except as it related to work. I was vocal there because that was the easiest place to lay the blame. But the truth of the matter is, for a while my life was in shambles because I made poor choices. And it wasn't until I accepted full responsibility for the state of my life that it began to change. The change wasn't immediate or overnight, but it has been continual.

As I've changed from the inside out, the need to hide has diminished. My ability to stand for what I want and believe has improved. My willingness to stand for others emerging.

Invincibility is being too powerful to be defeated. My invincibility comes from who I am and whose I am. As a child of God, I am unstoppable because I chose to be who I was created to be. I am unstoppable because the poor choices I've made, or my failures, don't define me or my worth. My worth is a gift from God. It's the same gift you have.

And despite all I've been through, self-created or not, I'm still standing, still thriving and still making a difference with my time, talents and treasures. I'm still loving, serving and giving. I'm still leading by example.

Being invincible is not about being a survivor, but rather a thriver. Living your best life. I've had my share of failures, disappointments, hurts and hang-ups. There were times when I felt I couldn't or didn't want to take another breath. The pain in those moments so unbearable that continuing seemed an unimaginable option. But in each of those moments, despite what I was feeling, the Holy Spirit intervened and kept me from making irreversible decisions.

My first memorable experience with the Holy Spirit happened about 20 years ago. It was a tangible experience in which I was so aware I knew the trajectory of my life shifted while in the midst of it.

I was out running one morning, as I had many mornings before and since. At that time, I was in pain. I was stuck in a recurring loop that had persisted far too long. I'd gone through a nasty divorce and custody battle that yielded no winners. Even though I hadn't learned or exercised the art of forgiveness yet, I thought I was good.

And other people thought I was good. I'd graduated law school and was working as a lawyer and lobbyist. To the outside world it looked like I had it all together. That's the funny thing about invisibility, people can see what you do and confuse that for who you are, making you totally unseen. That's where I was.

So, as I stepped out of my house that morning, I was crying about my life. How unhappy I was. How I couldn't get anything right. Asking what was wrong with me. Why I was in so much pain. The more I asked, the more I cried. As the tears continued to stream from my eyes and snot ran from my nose, I was in the middle of the street and could barely catch my breath. In all of that, I heard a voice say, "Try me. You've never given me a try. Try me."

That voice, one I'd never heard before, or at least listened to, caught my attention. While I didn't know quite what to do with it at that time, I knew I would never be the same. In the weeks and months that followed, I began to develop a relationship with God that before that day I didn't even know was possible.

The real reason I am invincible has nothing to do with me, except to the extent my choices have led me to this relationship that fills the God-sized holes in my soul with His love and acceptance. I knew I was invincible when I managed to survive the darkest time of my life. It was two years after my side of the road encounter with God that this incident rocked my world.

In June 2005, while driving home from his high school graduation, my son fell asleep at the wheel of his car and crashed into a grove of eucalyptus trees. He and one of his passengers died as a result of their injuries. For the weeks and months following, I was barely alive myself as I tried to come to grips with the devastating loss. But for my relationship with God, I would not have survived the pain.

The turnaround on living my life fully started on that morning run. It gathered steam after my son died. And it was full speed ahead when I decided to walk away from the job that was killing my spirit.

God did not create me with a spirit of timidity or fear, but of power and love. His power, His love. He has given me His power and the ability to draw on it anytime I need. For far too long I tried to do everything in my own power and was constantly feeling put upon and a victim.

So, I started sharing my story. Not just the part that would elicit sympathy, but the failures. The mistakes. A funny thing happened on my journey of sharing, the real me has flourished. There is nothing to hide. Have I shared everything? Not yet, but it's coming. There is a right time, place and audience for every story.

Invisibility was a choice. For me it was a protection mechanism. Invincibility, too, is a choice. A choice made because the alternative was a nonstarter. I thought because I spent my life out there, not physically hiding, not afraid to speak up, that meant I was being seen and heard. But the truth is as long as I was lurking in the shadows, I wasn't living authentically. And it wasn't until I decided to step into the light, to be fully seen, that I was able to step into my power and be invincible.

Contributor Biographies

The contributors would love to hear from you! For a link to contact them, go to:

www.InvincibleForeverMore.com

 **Lynda Sunshine West** is known as The Fear Buster. She's a Speaker, 6 times Bestselling Author, Executive Film Producer, Red Carpet Interviewer, and the Founder of Women Action Takers. Women Action Takers' mission is to empower 5 million women to find, use, and AMPLIFY their voice on paper, on video, and on stage. At age 51 she faced one fear every day for an entire year. In doing so, she gained an exorbitant amount of confidence and uses what she learned to fulfill her mission by giving women from all over the world the opportunity to share their voice. She believes in cooperation and collaboration and loves connecting with like-minded people.

You can connect with Lynda Sunshine here: https://womenactiontakers.com

 **Forbes Riley** is a Celebrity TV Host, Health and Fitness Expert, Entrepreneur, Visionary.

Forbes mesmerizes audiences with her authentic, inspirational style that is second to none. Often referred to as Oprah meets Tony Robbins, she transports, transforms and transfixes audiences from 100 to 10,000.

As one of the pioneers behind the As Seen on TV infomercial phenomenon, Forbes Riley has hosted 180+ infomercials and guested on QVC/HSN with more than 350 products generating more than $2.5 billion in global sales. Twenty of her shows (including Jack LaLanne Juicer, Montel Williams Healthmaster) have each exceeded $100 million in revenue.

As a health and fitness expert, Forbes was inducted into the National Fitness Hall of Fame and is the creator and CEO of the fitness phenomenon, SpinGym. The product alone has sold more than 2 million units and she has a team of worldwide Brand Ambassadors promoting workplace wellness to major corporations.

"When you're looking for a speaker to TRANSFORM your audience so they leave feeling better about themselves but talking about you… Forbes Riley, she's the one!"
– Les Brown, Motivational Speaker

You can connect with Forbes at http://www.forbesriley.com

Rachele Brooke Smith is an actress, host, coach, and motivational speaker seen frequently on Hollywood screens, modeling for major brands, and motivating fans around the world.

After playing the lead in the sequel to the film that changed her life as a little girl (Center Stage) and literally doing what everyone told her was impossible, Rachele is on a mission to empower others to create #HeroHabits, disrupt doubt, and become the hero of their own life story.

Since her breakout lead role in Center Stage: Turn It Up, she has been in countless films and TV shows like "Bring It On," "Nice Guys," "Burlesque," "Iron Man 2," "How I Met Your Mother," "Two and A Half Men," "Atomic Shark," "Scream Queens," "Class Act," Lifetime's: "Psycho Stripper" and "My Sister's Deadly Secret," and has several that are soon to be released, including a new Inspirational film, "Be The Light," a new comedy, "In Other Words," her lead role, opposite Danny Trejo, in "The Last Exorcist," and the film she is currently working on, a powerful psychological thriller that is a timely, relevant (#Metoo) film, you won't want to miss, "The Method." She is playing "Iris" who is the leader of the rebels, creating a mass amount of positive rebellion, in her new action series she is producing and starring in called, "The Legend of the White Dragon."

Rachele also lights up the stage, and or screen, as a host. She has hosted world-renowned events like the "Start Up World Cup" 4 years in a row and she is committed to helping elevate the human consciousness and spread her philosophy of using "The 5C Hero Habits" curiosity, creativity, compassion, courage, & connection along with empowering music, movements, mindsets, and movies as tools to help disrupt doubt, fear, and or limiting beliefs and help people become the hero of their own life's story.

In addition, Rachele and her partner, Emilio Palafox, co-created their media company, Relationship Renegades, and co-host one of the best new relationship radio shows, Relationship Renegades. Their mission is to help people learn how to "Kill their Superman to find their Wonder Woman" and co-create a world where healthy relationships are the new norm.

"Sick and tired of toxic, unhealthy relationships? We are too. We believe that regardless of the challenges you have faced in your past, it's still possible to create the love and lifestyle you've always wanted. And, we're here to help you do that! @TheRelationshipRenegades"

Listen to Relationship Renegades Radio show everyone week on Fun For Life Radio Channel on Dash Radio.

You can connect with Rachele here: https://rachelebsmith.com

Amy Morrison's mission is to coach Entrepreneurship to women who are coming from an emotional/mental and/or physically abusive relationship and sex trafficking Survivors, who need empowerment and confidence to know they can provide for themselves and their children. She brings women out of the shadows into their Power.

Amy is passionate about fundraising to empower women in the USA and other countries who are coming out of abuse and Human/Sex Trafficking. They learn a dignified trade that empowers them to provide for their children and themselves.

Women/Artisians make jewelry, scarves, handbags, journals, soap and even a coffee plantation in Antigua that ships their coffee to buyers directly from their plantation.

It is truly a triple win for the women who are now thriving instead of surviving, empowering them to make a difference for those who are blessed by your organization, and your participating contributors will be a part of making a difference for your organization and women around the world.

You can connect with Amy here: https://linktr.ee/amymorrison.empowerherpower

With over 30 years of experience in tours and travel management, **Angelica Waite** has a deep appreciation for responsible travel. Tourism brings remarkable and authentic adventures, profit for businesses, benefits to locals, and is kind to the natural environment.

As the Managing Director of Advantage Eco Trails and Events in Nairobi, Kenya, Angelica provides tours for people all over the world.

You can connect with Angelica here: http://advantagecotrails.co.ke/

Betty Morin lives in Francis, Utah, with her husband, two boys, dogs and cats. As a seasoned teacher and practitioner of yoga and meditation, her passion is to rest in the present and share tools with others that she has honed - especially youth and parents! She does this through writing, public speaking, working with small groups and individuals. In her free time, she loves to play outside year-round, especially hiking, snowmobiling, and trying new outdoor activities; playing helps her stay in the gift of the present moment!

You can connect with Betty here: https://www.moveinwarduplift.com

Bridgetti Lim Banda is a Remote Live TV Producer and talk show host who leads conversations with brands and thought leaders. She started her livestreaming career raising awareness about the Cape Town water crisis in South Africa and was featured several times on international tv and radio in recognition of her work. She is an active member of the global livestreaming community. Bridgetti was the first person on the African continent to be granted access to livestream on LinkedIn Live, which is the largest business platform in the world. She has also been recognised as a Global Goodwill Ambassador.

You can connect with Bridgetti here: http://www.blivemedia.com

Cathy Derksen is the founder of Inspired Tenacity. She is dedicated to improving the lives of the women in her community. She transformed her career from working as a lab technologist into financial planning so she could focus her energy on helping others in a more direct manner.

After digging deeper into her innate drive to be of service, she added another level to her connection within her community. Cathy now provides online resources to assist women in discovering their deeper calling by adjusting their mindset and focus in order to reach their goals.

She helps women clarify their next step and apply courage and inspired tenacity to live the life that brings them joy. Cathy is a 2-time #1 bestselling author with more books being released soon with stories that inspire the reader to take a leap of faith into reaching for their big goals.

You can connect with Cathy here: https://inspiredtenacity.com

Cecilia Rankin is the founder of Health Coaching 4ever. She loves adventure. Beware, she will say "yes" if you tell her about one. Her motto is "Life is full of field trips, so go on them before it's too late!"

Her life field trips have included summiting Mount Kilimanjaro, trekking to basecamp Everest, climbing Devil's Tower and Half Dome.

She is an elementary school teacher who will do whatever it takes for all students to succeed.

Coaching people over the age of 40 & 50 to get their health back, she helps them manage type 2 diabetes, chronic joint pains, lower their bad cholesterol, get rid of constant food cravings, fatigue and unwanted weight.

You can connect with Cecilia here: https://chooseyourpathwithcecyourcoach.now.site

Dr. Christine Sauer provides Health Consultation, Education, and Coaching Services around the 5 Dimensions of Health to optimize the Quality of Life of Individuals. The founder, Dr. Christine Sauer, is a German-trained, now retired, conventional and naturopathic physician with over 30 years of experience. At DocChristine, we offer a unique and unified perspective of whole-person health and wellness.

You can connect with Dr. Christine here: https://docchristine.com

Delores Garcia, MS, CPT, CLC, is a retired nutrition professor who now guides her coaching clients in reprogramming their mind for unprecedented personal success. Most people have goals, yet also have a push-pull tug-of-war with negative mind chatter: old, recycled, habitual thoughts that are actually blocking the path to abundant health, wealth, and happiness. Using her "Empowered Mindset Method," Delores helps them re-wire their Operating System (aka subconscious mind) to accomplish their goals in Flow, while enjoying incredible work/life satisfaction. She uses a simple, yet powerful, science-based tool that builds new neural pathways in minutes, removing those pesky mental blocks, and forever altering the trajectory of her clients' life.

You can connect with Delores here: https://deloresgarciacoaching.now.site

Kristy Boyd Johnson is the Boss Lady at Turtle Sea Books. She is the author of more than 30 books, holds an MFA in Screenwriting, is a recovering school teacher, and loves writing children's books. Her favorite pastimes are swimming, long walks, and reading a great book.

You can connect with Kristy here: www.TurtleSeaBooks.com.

Krysten Maracle is the founder of Maracle Mastermind. She invested 35 years as a civilian at Naval Information Warfare Center Pacific in San Diego, California, working in various roles: Computer Scientist, Program Manager, Contracting Officer Representative and retired in December 2019. She supports the Wounded Warrior Project in San Diego, is an Executive Producer of Wish

Man Movie, and founding member of the Mastermind Association. Krysten's passions are encouraging people to overcome their trauma as well as traveling the world.

You can connect with Krysten here: https://www.facebook.com/krysten.maracle

Simply put, **Krystylle Richardson** loves seeing people become better versions of themselves mentally, physically, spiritually, financially, emotionally and more. Krystylle believes that she was personally put on this earth by God to help people evict mind-trash and cancel mediocrity. She played small in portions of her life for years. That feeling sucked, so she did something about it. She believes that we all have greatness and we can activate God's favor if we just move out of our own way.

Krystylle's focus is helping women as a Wealth Innovation Coach. She helps them identify their real purpose, increase streams of income and media exposure so they can Be Heard, Be Great & Get Paid.

She is the energized creator of The Woman Weekend-Preneur™ and is the ICN Global Ambassador of Innovation. Krystylle has 35 years of experience in international business. Her faith and unique skillsets have produced countless testimonials and her being given the name "The Untapped Income Coach."

Krystylle is an International Speaker - Leadership and Mindset Accountability Coach - International Bestselling Author - TV & Radio Show Host - Red Carpet Interviewer - Philanthropist - an Awarded Humanitarian - Missionary - Genetic Research Engineer & Exec - Wife and Mother.

She has been featured in USA Today, NBC, CBS, Think & Grow Rich Legacy World Tour, Hollywood Glam and coming soon in Yahoo! Finance. She believes that after self-acceptance, she knows for a fact that the possibilities are endless. Krystylle's superpower is RELENTLESS TENACITY and living out loud.

You can connect with Krystylle here: www.KrystylleRichardson.com.

 **Legend Thurman** is a DVM Candidate at the Royal Veterinary College in London, England. As a Catholic University of America graduate, originally from Washington, PA and Washington, DC, Legend aspires to be a full-time governmental veterinarian after graduation advocating for change in veterinary medicine in legislation, public policy, and advocacy.

She has served as a Delegate for RVC on National SAVMA's House of Delegates, National SAVMA's Governmental Affairs Committee Chair, and is currently the RVC SAVMA Chapter President. During Covid-19, she formed a Covid-19 Hardship Grant for students and helped write new legislation alongside other students for the National SAVMA By-Laws to alter membership guidelines for student chapters who have been affected by various disasters. Her focus is on advancing exposure to students on issues such as well-being, DEI, organized medicine, one health, and relationships in the field.

Legend's roots align with that of servant leadership from her Catholic faith that has helped shape who she is today along with her life's motto: "God, Family, and Veterinary Medicine."

You can connect with Legend here:
https://www.linkedin.com/in/legend-thurman

 **Mary Elizabeth Jackson** is the 2017 Gold Maxy award-winning author of the children's book series *Perfectly Precious Poohlicious, Poohlicious Look at Me,* and *Poohlicious Oh the Wonder of Me* (Tuscany Bay Books). *Cheers from Heaven,* a mid-grade reader releases late 2021 (Tuscany Bay Books), with co-writer Thornton Cline. Jackson focuses on writing empowering books for kids. Jackson is also a ghostwriter, book collaborator, and the voice for the Sports2Gether app.

Mrs. Jackson is a special needs advocate and an Ambassador Advocate for AutismTn. She co-founded and co-hosts Writers Corner Live TV and Special Needs TV Shows that air on Amazon Live, Facebook, Twitter, LinkedIn, and YouTube. Writers Corner Live features author interviews and all things in the writing world. Special Needs TV features interviews and resources for parents, families, and caregivers. Jackson is also working on an edutainment YouTube channel with her son featuring children's book reviews and family fun and education.

You can connect with Mary here: www.MaryEJackson.com.

 **Melodie Donovan** is an IT Professional of 20 years, a bartender for 6, and a serial entrepreneur for 11. Melodie recently launched her financial coaching business to help women with their journey to financial freedom. She is a Certified Financial Coach through Ramsey Financial Coaching. She also recently became a travel agent and Traveling Vineyards Wine guide to learn more about wine, meet other people, and enjoy some wine along the way.

You can connect with Melodie here: https://MelodieInc.com

Mischelle O'Neal is the Founder of Mastering Your Monday, LLC, a Lifestyle Enrichment Firm based out of Northern Virginia. She's an author, speaker, podcast host, and certified life coach who is excited about serving those who are passionate about efficiently pursuing their purpose in life.

Her business was inspired by a desire to help those who carry a deep commitment and responsibility towards the things and people they love to find the way to thrive in an environment where their passions, personal lives, and professional aspirations can co-exist. She prides herself on helping them find a way to manage the constant tug-of-war and get rid of the guilt which can materialize from the overwhelming demands that can exist. Mischelle guides them on the journey to finding a better way of bringing balance and control back into their lives.
She specializes in assisting these amazing individuals in developing a more balanced, productive, and fulfilling lifestyle. As a result of working with her, they gain a healthier work/life balance, increase their efficiency and influence, and learn to acknowledge their true value.

You can connect with Mischelle here: https://masteringyourmonday.com

Mistie Layne is an Empowerment and Resiliency expert transforming lives by helping release toxic beliefs to overcome any adversity with confidence and resilience. Mistie overcame her worst to live her best by realizing her past was robbing her future and decided to take control of her own life. She is now a bestselling author of her life story, *What Goes Up*, and claims writing was the therapy that saved her life while sitting in a prison facing a forty-year sentence. When you learn more about Mistie, you will be inspired to adopt a positive mentality by realizing you are now an authority on the other side of your adversity and can use your knowledge to help others.

You can connect with Mistie here: www.StepUpAndSpeakOut.com.

 **Nancy Lockhart** leverages her 20 years of experience creating iconic brands with law of attraction life coaching to help female business owners rebrand themselves in order to become more profitable, successful, and full of purpose. Unlock the heart of your business with Lockhart Marketing.

You can connect with Nancy here: https://lockhart-marketing.com

 Physically, emotionally and spiritually exhausted after a lifetime of yo-yo dieting, **Paige Davidson** began a journey in search of something different: true healing. Her unique journey began with Christian counseling, and the discovery of Intermittent Fasting (IF), a healthy method of alternating eating food within a period of time with clean fasting on a daily basis.

Paige lost an astounding 110 pounds, healed several health conditions, was featured on the cover of Woman's World magazine, and wrote *Fast With Paige: Health & Healing Practices for Forever Freedom*, available on Amazon.

This spiritual journey with physical healing led Paige to a deep calling to help as many women like her as possible. She has coached, inspired, and mentored thousands of Intermittent Fasters virtually throughout the world.

Through this work, Paige recognized the need for successful IF lifestyle coaches who are supportive, knowledgeable about coaching, and dedicated to client success. She proactively completed an Integrative Health & Wellness Coach certification to bolster her strengths and experience in working with adult learners as a trainer and communications professional for the state of Kentucky.

Armed with experience, certification, and success in losing significant weight through IF, she began a private virtual coaching business called Fast-Track Health & Wellness.

You can connect with Paige here: http://www.thefastingpaige.com

 **Pamela Gort's** mission is to help lesbians create real transformation for their highest good so they attract a conscious relationship with the woman of their dreams. Awaken the Love Within so You can Awaken the Love Outside. She brings humor, play and curiosity into coaching sessions, training and speaking.

After a phenomenally successful 30-year career in Pharma and Biotech, Pamela completely changed gears and went back to what she loved – relationship coaching as well as inspirational speaking.

Trained by Christian Mickelsen, known as the Coach to Coaches, Pamela is certified as a Relationship Coach, Positive Intelligence Coach, and Hilton Johnson Health Coach. She teaches and utilizes Instant Miracle, the Peace Process and Mental Fitness modalities to help her center and ground her clients so they can focus on love and finally attract a better version of happily ever after.

Pamela is the proud mother of two daughters and lover of sunsets, especially at the beach. Pamela's interest in coaching started when she volunteered for 5 years with Contact Crisis Counseling Hotline. She facilitates workshops, one-on-one and group coaching.

You can connect with Pamela here: https://lesbianrelationshipcoach. com

Sally Green is the founder of The Self-Care Rockstar, empowering people to begin a regime of self-care for healthy living. She is a Christian educator, artist, and a 2-time international best-selling author. Sally has also written two Bible studies and an inspirational book of poetry.

You can connect with Sally here: www.TheSelfCareRockstar.com.

Sarah Jung is an author, a speaker, a certified master coach of NLP, Timeline Therapy, and Hypnotherapy, a serial entrepreneur, an educator, and a lifelong student.

She is the biological mother of two, and a guardian mother of many international students she hosts. She's also a black belt in Taekwondo, a piano player, a coffee addict, and lives in San Diego, CA.

After her 9-year marriage ended in 2013, she found herself in the valley, searching for answers, and discovered the version of herself that she had been hiding, silenced and invisible. Breaking out of her shell, she set out on a mission to share her story, to speak up, and to be "Not Invisible on Purpose."

You can connect with Sarah here: www.SarahIsMyCoach.com

Sherri Leopold is a mentor, 3 times International Bestselling Author, Speaker, Founder and CEO of Dream Big with Sherri Leopold. She is a Dr. Amen Licensed Brain Health Trainer and enjoys teaching on the topic of brain health. She is a television host of the show *Outside the Box with Sherri Leopold* on Legrity.TV. She has worked in the Network Marketing/Direct Selling industry as a top producer for 24 years, sharing her expertise in speaking, mentoring, and team building.

Sherri released her first book in June of 2019 called Self-Bullying: What To Do When the Bully is YOU! As Leader of the Stop Self-Bullying Movement, Sherri has a membership program called War On Words (WOW) Warriors. This Stop Self-Bullying training helps eradicate negative self-talk and teaches people to Stand UP and Stand OUT as the unrepeatable miracle they are!! She has designed a Facebook support group called WOW Warriors to encourage self-love and create a place of love and encouragement.

You can connect with Sherri here: www.SherriLeopold.com.

Suz deMello says, "I'm a cliche...A vegan yoga teacher from California who loves walks on the beach, cuddling her dogs and romance novels." But she's an award-winning, best-selling writer of 24 books who's hit several best-seller lists, been short-listed for the RITA and reviewed by such prestigious publications such as Kirkus, Library Journal and Publisher's Weekly.

Her personal motto is: Never stop learning, never stop growing. She's had at least six careers she can remember: librarian, trial attorney, Starbucks barista, grant writer, ESL teacher and yoga instructor. She's also earned a 2d degree black belt in Kenpo karate.

She currently resides in Mexico, where she practices yoga, cuddles her dogs and walks on the beach every day. And she's still writing romance.

You can connect with Suz here: www.suzdemello.com

Trayce Young is a mindset and victory coach. She empowers women to shift from negative thinking to having a positive mindset so they may see their dreams come to fruition and walk in purpose. It is her passion to help women make transformational changes so they may live victoriously.

You can connect with Trayce here: trayce.young@lrsd.org

After the death of her son and finding it difficult to say out loud much  of what she was experiencing, **Whitnie Wiley**'s journey as an author began by her chronicling her grief journey.

Since those painful early days, Whitnie has shared her words on leadership and career management with hundreds of thousands of readers around the world as the author for the Lead the Way column in the Association of Corporate Counsel's Docket magazine. She encouraged her readers to develop self-awareness and use their values and priorities to pave their path to enjoying their careers, better leadership, and improved teamwork.

As an in-demand coach, speaker, and mentor, Whitnie shares her wisdom from her own life experiences with grace, humility, and humor to drive change in today's business world. Combining her passions for writing, accountability, and coaching, Whitnie helps new and aspiring writers complete their writing projects and get published through her Writers Write Accountability Group and one-on-one coaching.

You can connect with Whitnie here: https://shiftingintoaction.now.site.

CPSIA information can be obtained
at www.ICGtesting.com
Printed in the USA
LVHW040554280821
696211LV00001B/9